KITTY

An Uncommon Memoir of a Non-celebrity

KITTY

An Uncommon Memoir of a Non-celebrity

Katherine M. Ruttenberg

Nelson-Hall nh Chicago

Library of Congress Cataloging in Publication Data

Ruttenberg, Katherine.
 Kitty, an uncommon memoir of a non-celebrity.

 Includes index.
  1. Ruttenberg, Katherine. 2. Jews in Pittsburgh—Biography. 3. Israel—Emigration and
immigration—Biography. 4. Pittsburgh—Biography. I Title.
 F159.P69J57 974.8'86'004924 [B] 79-21057
 ISBN 0-88229-654-X

Manufactured in the United States of America

10   9   8   7   6   5   4   3   2   1

Contents

To Harold:
my partner in a lifetime of shared experiences and ideas; my fellow traveler in love, time and space.

Preface

When, upon my father's death, I became the oldest of three generations, my spirits plunged. I fell into reflection on the past and contemplation of the present—and into moments of depression that lasted days and weeks and months at a time. Always anniversary conscious and milestone minded, I now saw dates and events of my life in bold relief: my mother's death fifteen years before (a permanent void); my arrival in America nearly half a century earlier (a new life for me); marriage and children (happiness, some frustrations and great challenges); my first trip abroad (I haven't been the same since); family gatherings and family excursions (filled with laughter and happy times); the children's weddings (beautiful dreams); my sixtieth birthday (an elegant fiasco); and, in two more years, the fortieth anniversary of my marriage (a remarkable achievement to anticipate).

It was time for emotional stocktaking, for setting the accounts in order. What were my regrets and disappointments? What gave me the most pleasure and happiness? Enjoying one's blessings and coping with one's grief are both elements of everyone's lifetime. What will my portions be from now on?

Phases of my life flashed by in a rich pageantry of cast and scenes; the players spoke to me in a chorus of several tongues and in many moods. The stage was filling up; the script was in its final act; emotions were spilling over.

Family life, from both a contemporary and a generational perspective, is a paradox: it consists of a chain of individual wonders, fashioned of links that are temporary; yet the intermeshed whole endures. The links pass on; the chain remains. To me, more important are the things that bind us than those that separate us.

Strains in the chain of which I am now the oldest link have been occurring in recent years. Are they reparable? Is the trend reversible? I can only speculate, hope, and pray. A sure remedy I cannot offer. In any case, I write these pages, chronicling the many happy phases and faces of my uncommon life story as comfort in moments of distress and as a reasonable basis for my fond expectations. I write in all candor and with deep devotion, love, and affection for my children, who may some day ask the questions this book attempts to answer.

Pittsburgh, Pennsylvania
1979

Acknowledgments

I am grateful to the late Viscount Edwin Samuel, friend for many years both in Pittsburgh and in Jerusalem, who kindly went through the whole typescript with me. Having himself written an autobiography, he was well qualified to advise me on mine.

Harold was supportive all the way; I appreciate his constant encouragement. My ancestors, my descendants and the people whose lives touched mine all have a pivotal role to play in my recollections, as they did in the direction my life has taken. A symbolic bow to all of them. They make my life worth living and my book real.

I am indebted to Stuart Brent, whose singular idea made his contribution invaluable. Carol Rausch Gorski, editor for Nelson-Hall, was extremely helpful in the final stages of the project. My special thanks to Freda Leff, friend of long standing, for her patience and countless hours in typing innumerable versions of all my material until I was satisfied with the final one.

Chapter 1

Family Background

The people on my father's side of the family far outnumber those on my mother's, both in the number of children in each generation and in the number of generations that I can trace. Father's great-grandfather, Simcha Manheim, was born in Hungary and died in 1838. Simcha's son, Latzko, died at sixty-eight when my father, his grandson, was a boy of six. Latzko's second wife, my great-grandmother, was Julia Diamant, a cousin of Theodor Herzl' mother. Thus, through her, I am related to a giant in Jewish history, the father of political Zionism.

Except for the aforementioned Simcha and Latzko, as well as my paternal grandparents, all the Manheims who preceded me enjoyed or endured, as the case may be, exceptionally long lives. Even at that, grandfather Leopold, who died in New York City in 1919, in his seventies, was no youngster. Nor was my grandmother, his cousin Jeanette Preisich; she was sixty-two when she died in 1920. Jeanette's four sisters lived on into their eighties. My father and his two sisters whom fate allowed to live out their years naturally died in their nineties.

My grandmother's oldest sister was Tante Tici (from Katica, a diminutive of the Hungarian version of Katherine), after whom I was named. Grandmother herself, who was living in New York when I was born, played the piano charmingly and spoke flawless

1

German and halting Hungarian. Neither she nor my other grandmother spoke Yiddish, though undoubtedly Yiddish phrases and expletives spiced their language on demand. In later years, grandmother Manheim also acquired enough English to manage life in America. On a recent visit to Czechoslovakia, my cousin Paul Monori and I made a special pilgrimage to the spot where our grandmother died. While she was on holiday in the world famous spa of Carlsbad, escaping fumes in her hotel room asphyxiated her while she was writing a letter to one of her children.

Grandfather Manheim's original business in Hungary was in dry goods. It somehow evolved into a firm dealing in wholesale spirits, the warehouse of which was government bonded. His last enterprise, which he operated with his eldest son, Armin, was Leopold Manheim and Son, an alcohol refinery that provided a comfortable living for the large and growing family. In the early 1900s, however, hard times struck. Profits were next to nil, competition was keen, and debts became overwhelming. Though their credit rating was good, bankruptcy was the best way out of their financial difficulties. After they settled their affairs in 1905, Leopold and Son made their way to America, where there was already a Manheim, grandfather's brother Sigmund. Armin's small family followed shortly, and lastly came my grandmother, who was accompanied by my father, Emil, then twenty-six years old. The saga of Uncle Armin in the new world from struggles to riches is a fascinating story by itself, but it doesn't belong in this account except to say that (1) it occasioned Father's first sojourn in America between 1906 and 1909 and (2) it explains the presence of a numerous clan of Manheims in New York, my American cousins.

In their student days at the Royal Technical University of Budapest, Father and his two brothers became enthusiastic Hungarian patriots; to show their displeasure with Austrian political domination and demonstrate their Hungarian identity, they changed their name to Monori—a choice based on euphony—when the youngest brother finished his studies. Uncle Joseph, who became an economist and government official, settled in that part of the country that became Czechoslovakia after World War I. Uncle Laszlo, a lawyer, became a Rumanian subject through a similar geographical accident. Two younger sisters, Aunt Gizella and Aunt Malvin, also lived in Transylvania, a province of Hungary that was ceded to Rumania by the Treaty of Trianon in 1920. They died in Israel in the 1970s.

Joseph, Laszlo, and their wives and children were deported to concentration camps shortly before the end of World War II. The two brothers and Laszlo's whole family suffered the tragic fate of 6 million fellow Jews. The sisters and their six children managed to survive. Through the years from the middle thirties to the late sixties, all were wise enough and fortunate enough to relocate in Israel, where I later became reacquainted with them. The earliest pioneer among my Israeli cousins was a dedicated Zionist at seventeen; the latest arrival is the cousin who fled with her family from Bratislava (Pozsony/Pressburg), Czechoslovakia, after Dubcek's fall in 1968.

Father was always willing and ready to speak of his past. The older he got, the richer were his reminiscences. From his account, I know that in his parents' home kashrut[1] was kept and all Jewish holidays were observed. The children all received their basic Jewish education; all the brothers were Bar Mitzvah. The family home was in Zolyom in (then) Upper Hungary, a town of eight thousand in the Carpathian Mountains on the main rail line between Budapest and Berlin. My father never had a desire to return to his native town; he derived enormous pleasure, however, from visits to Budapest, the scene of his student days and young manhood. Frank Manheim, a New York cousin now living in London, did at one time make a sentimental journey to Zolyom and sent his Uncle Emil a picture postcard to prove it.

Father recalled his childhood in affectionate terms. His was a well-to-do bourgeois merchant family enjoying material comforts and plenty of household help and affording travel and education as well as payments to exempt the boys from military service.

In his middle teens Father attended gymnazium in a nearby small city and distinguished himself as a scholar, especially in mathematics and the classics. His native tongue was Hungarian, and he received his education in it; but he also knew some Slovak as a child, as this was the language of the servants and peasants. His German was flawless, his French quite adequate. His basic Latin was excellent, his Greek minimal. To the end of his days, he could quote the appropriate Latin proverb for any occasion and could dissect every English word with a Latin or Greek derivation. Of his high school subjects, mathematics became the basis from which his professional life flowed. In the Hungarian national mathematics contests for secondary school students, two names appear most prominently in the middle and late 1890s: Kármán Tivador and Manheim Emil. They alternated being in first or second place. Theodore von Kármán and Emil Monori never met, but Father was rather amused by the fact that his rival for honors later won fame as an American pioneer in aerodynamics.

Beginning in early adulthood, Father and his siblings became less and less outwardly religious and led lives more and more secular. The one exception was Gizella, in Jerusalem, who to the day of her death, lit Shabat candles with a traditional flair and utter sincerity. My father was the only one among his generation who seriously flirted with conscious assimilation, just short of conversion. This, strangely, was in America, when I was a teenager. I was his willing partner at first, but Mother's genuine sense of Jewish identity and her perseverance kept our flirtation innocuous and inconclusive. In his later years, in a curious turnabout, he participated in family celebrations of holidays and accompanied children and grandchildren to occasional religious services with enthusiastic tolerance. He glowed with pride, as we all did, when his grandson, Eddie, became a rabbi.

Father was awarded his engineering diploma from the University of Budapest in 1901. For the next five years, he worked as a mechanical and electrical engineer with Ganz and Co., the largest heavy machinery manufacturing company in Hungary. However, still unmarried, he was either restless, bored, or merely anxious for adventure. In any case, he left for America in 1906, accompanying his mother. His father and older brother were already in New York City, but he settled in Schenectady, where employment as an engineer was offered. He had a commendable knowledge of English and had no professional or personal problems during the three years he was with General Electric. He might have stayed on, and this narrative might never have been written. But three years later, fate decreed otherwise. He yielded to family pressure to return to Transylvania, where the sisters and their husbands were engaged in the manufacturing of "Irish" handmade laces and trimmings that formed the European half of the Manheim import-export business. The laces were, of course, made by the Hungarian and Rumanian peasant women of the province; they were all the rage in the world of high fashion everywhere. Emil was to lend his talents to the expansion of the business, making it even more profitable. Father, however, had no entrepreneurial skills, and his association with the Hungarian American Lace Export Company hastened its downfall.

In the still "good old times" year of 1912, he was the personification of an eligible young man for a well-brought-up young woman with good family connections and a respectable dowry. By then he had given up laces; but not without considerable financial strain to himself. He was again employed at Ganz and Company. There was every reason to think that he was on the threshold of a fine career and could offer the right girl an interesting and secure life. In Budapest in 1912, Ilonka (Helen) Fein and Emil Monori were right for each other.

Mother could trace her family only back to her grandfather. Born early in the first decade of the nineteenth century, Moses was the first Jew who was allowed to own land in his province. In the third decade of that new century he carried a surname that his father had acquired in the 1790s. Under the terms of an Emancipation Ordinance for Jews, by the enlightened Hapsburg monarch Joseph II, Moses's father, being a very fine man indeed, was officially named Fein. This is how legend has it, and Mother was always fiercely proud of her name, as well as the legend surrounding its acquisition.

My maternal grandparents lived in a large, rambling country house north of Budapest on an extensive tract of land that they owned; their own peasants cultivated it. Grandfather was also entrusted with the management of a large estate owned by the aristocrat Daruvary. From this he derived a percentage of the yield and the friendship of an influential patron, who was also a member of Parliament. The land was good to the Feins: he supervised the peasants ably, and the family prospered. Household help was plentiful, and the three children were given an excellent education. They were tutored at home in the early years. Later, the son, Eugene, was sent to secondary school and then to an academy of commerce and finance; the daughters attended a girls' boarding school in a nearby larger town, the county seat Aszod. Mother and Aunt Aranka were instructed through their teens in all academic subjects and trained in the domestic skills that were the desirable attributes of all young ladies of a good family. Music and art, both fine and applied, were my mother's accomplishments throughout her life. Uncle Gene entered banking and later dabbled in the stock exchange. An eccentric bachelor, he died in deplorable circumstances in his early sixties from a massive cerebral hemorrhage. Ironically, we were at this time in the midst of arrangements to bring him to America under the auspices of ourselves and cousin Klari's (his only other next of kin besides my mother).

Attached to my grandparents' house was a small private chapel where religious services for Shabat and major holidays were held for Jewish families scattered over the tri-county area and for itinerant peddlars. Grandfather Laszlo Fein was not a rabbi, but he apparently had enough knowledge to provide for the needs of his fellow Jews. He also secured a rabbi for High Holydays and made arrangements for religious functions relating to life cycle milestones. He possessed all the accoutrements for religious rites and, to this day in Pittsburgh, Pennsylvania, a sacred Torah scroll and an Esther's *Megillah* speak eloquently of those faraway and bygone days in the Hungarian village of Erdötarcsa. In an impressive Shabat Eve ceremony in Pittsburgh's Temple Sinai (December, 1957), this Torah scroll was dedicated in the presence of my parents, our four children, ourselves, and a large congregation.

Grandfather Fein died in 1910 at the age of sixty-seven from complications of a urinary malfunction. Grandmother Fein died ten years later at the age of fifty-seven, from cancer of the liver. At that time my parents secured two documents from the Jewish Community secretariat, listing their parents' *yahrzeits* for the next twenty-five years. Handsomely decorated with Biblical scenes, these documents show correct Hebrew dates and corresponding dates by day of the week, month, and year in the civil calendar of the anniversaries of their deaths.

Mother's mother, neé Minna Schäfer, was much younger than her husband and more sophisticated. She was well read and kept up with events of the day. She often took the "cure" in Carlsbad. She yearned for the big city, and, during the "season," she and her daughters maintained a small pied-à-terre in Budapest, several hours' from Erdötarcsa by coach and train. There was nothing provincial about these Fein women. They took to musical, theatrical and operatic events with much gusto. During one of these seasons, the older daughter met her future husband, a talented commercial artist. Two years later, in 1912, my parents met through a mutual friend.

Mother was then in her mid-twenties, lively and attractive. She entertained some unconventional ideas and came to the marriage with a good dowry. Father was a mature thirty-two, handsome and a professional man who had seen something of the world (the brief American interlude). He had also incurred some debts in behalf of his family (the lace fiasco), which he paid off gradually after his marriage. Their known qualities seemed to mesh ideally.

I find the following dedication (in Hungarian of course) in *Mirjam*, a book of prayers for Jewish women that Father gave Mother on occasion of the approaching High Holydays in 1913: "During your prayers, while seeking solace in times of trouble or sorrow, or giving thanks to the Almighty in times of joy and happiness, may you think of me, your ever-adoring husband whose every thought is inspired by his innermost feelings of love and devotion for you." Since my mother's death, *Mirjam* is always with me, even on my travels.

My parents took their honeymoon in Vienna, Munich and Paris and Venice. From this period I still have the formal wedding photograph taken in Vienna and an exquisite pair of mother-of-pearl-in-mosaic opera glasses he bought for her in Paris. I was negligent in not learning more about the wedding, but this much I remember Mother telling me: she rebelled against following the formal religious ceremony her sister had had two years before and insisted on a simple civil ceremony—May 13, 1913—attended only by a dozen members of their respective families who lived in Budapest.

Chapter 2

A Far Childhood

Fact and fancy, positive recollection and nostalgia—all these combine to form childhood memories. In relating the beginnings of my own life story, I start with an undisputable fact. I was born on May 18, 1914, in Budapest, twin capital with Vienna of the Austro-Hungarian Empire, as the first and only child of loving parents. They were no youngsters and didn't have to wait for me longer than the required one year.

It was a beautiful and peaceful spring. While diplomatic ultimatums and sword rattlings emanated from Serbia and Austria, life in Budapest's cafés and on the Corso (the promenade along the banks of the Danube) was unruffled by the headlines. Vienna and Berlin were angry and indignant, but no one in my parents' social set was as yet affected. War was altogether unthinkable.

My mother's private show of strength took place in the bedroom of a brand new modern apartment in a lovely middle-class neighborhood. After a day and a night in labor, she was delivered of an undersized, black-haired and black-eyed female baby—me. Mother discarded the romantic and flowery name she had picked in her girlhood—Portulaca—and they named me Katalin[2] Noemi (Katherine Naomi). Father was on the premises, supportive but helpless. Her doctor, an eminent professor, kept a

9

watchful eye on the accouchement, but, according to local custom of the times, was merely in readiness should the midwife need his professional expertise. No complications at birth; these were reserved for the war years ahead. Three and a half days later, a handsome, light-haired and light-complexioned baby boy was born to Fannie Weinstein and Charles Ruttenberg—sixty-three hundred miles and seven time zones away—in St. Joseph's Hospital, St. Paul, Minnesota, in the United States of America. Of this significant event I was blissfully ignorant at the time. Two decades and one world war later, however, our paths met and have been happily and fruitfully parallel ever since.

August, 1914. Father was called up for military duty but was exempted for a combination of reasons: medical grounds (flat feet) and because his employment in a defense industry was essential. During this time we simply hoped for an early, victorious end to hostilities. Father eventually did serve King and Emperor Franz Joseph and, later, Karl (the last reigning Hapsburg) as a noncommissioned officer. However, he promptly qualified for officers' training school and, in 1915, off he went for one course after another to prepare for active duty. Mother and I sometimes followed him to his military stations. Finally, as a second lieutenant and a trained telephone and telegraph communications officer, he was dispatched with his unit to the eastern front. At war's end, he was mustered out with the rank of first lieutenant and several medals for bravery. Decades later, my father often reminded us that he had foreseen the power struggles of the fifties; he fought the Russians long before the Americans were engaged in a cold war with them.

Mother's main concern with my feeding and general health was caused by the wartime absence of orange juice and cod liver oil. Later on, an even more unpleasant scarcity was that of basic foodstuffs: they simply disappeared from this grocery shelf or that open-air food stall. A black market flourished, and currency was counted by the millions. These hard times continued well after hostilities came to an end. The country had suffered a humiliating defeat at the hands of the Allies. The economy was seriously crippled by the dismemberment of the Austro-

Hungarian Empire. Revolution, counterrevolution, Reds and Whites followed one another with devastating impact on the social and political structure.

As for me, I was nursed and watched over in the relative safety of Budapest. Within the home and the narrow confines of family and friends, I grew up as a contented and well-adjusted child. For so I was described by my parents. I was also demonstrative and affectionate, as were my mother and father. To this day I fail to understand children, mine included, when they are not.

My earliest recollection is of walks with my father when I was three or four years old: when I tired, he would pick me up and carry me the rest of the way. We frequently took Margit Bridge to Margit Island in the Danube. Even earlier, he wheeled me around in my pram in broad daylight. This was most unconventional; a gentleman of his class just didn't do that! But then, he had been to America and had picked up strange ways. . . .

There was a considerable turnover of living-in maids in our household, the jill-of-all-trades variety who cleaned, did most of the cooking chores—Mother was actually the chief cook—carried up the ice, and ran sundry errands. There was also a weekly laundress who worked in the attic under the most unpleasant conditions of stale air, suffocating steam and total lack of labor-saving devices. When not otherwise engaged, the maid escorted me to and from the homes of playmates. When I was about four and a half, I acquired a "fräulein" who came to the house daily, taught me kindergarten skills and German, and took over the maid's task of escorting me around on foot or the trolley.

There were several fräuleins in my young life, their primary qualification for the position being their command of excellent German. They had to be from Vienna, and they had to be from "good" families because of their close contact with me. German is a language both my parents spoke and wrote well, and they believed in its value for me. Nevertheless, I lost this linguistic advantage. At home we never stopped speaking Hungarian even though English assumed an equal rank a very short time after we reached the United States. Mother learned to speak and write English extremely well, but with a charming accent. Total immersion in mastering English when I was a new immigrant in America is my excuse for losing German by the wayside. I wish I had tried just a little harder then; I would now be multilingual.

As it is, while German still has a familiar ring for me, I do not speak it. It is French I promote for myself, chiefly by my participation in a Friday afternoon reunion of seven friends who are equally interested in improving their conversation facility. Whether we lapse into English occasionally or not, we all charge and stimulate each other on many levels. My progress in Hebrew is discouragingly slow, being at a standstill of about four hundred words and phrases; I depend solely on osmosis for improvement.

At the age of ten I entered a *gymnazium*, in spite of the *Numerus Clausus* law that had been in effect since Rear Admiral Nicholas Horthy rode into Budapest on a white horse to save the city from the communists. A spiritual antecedent of the American quota system, the law applied mainly to Jewish university students, whose numbers were never to be more than a certain percentage of the total. Even those who were permitted to enroll didn't fare any too well, suffering cruel harassment and sometimes actual beatings. Getting into a state secondary school, such as mine, also became more difficult, although only the spirit of the law, not the law itself, prevailed. Nevertheless, high level *protekcia* was absolutely essential for the acceptance of a Jewish child. My father's comradeship in his youth with the school principal was all the pull we needed. And since I did exceptionally well in the qualifying examination, my name appeared high on the list of successful applicants. Jewish students with no connections, no matter what their score, were rejected— thus outside the "closed number." Just the same, about a third of the pupils in Maria Terezia Girls Gymnazium in the mid-twenties were Jewish—an unusually high percentage which speaks well for either the Jewish students' scholarship and/or their connections in high places.

As soon as my admission was assured, Father was obliged to leave for America. In fact, he couldn't have taken a later train in order to board his ship on time. And that ship was the last scheduled to arrive in the United States before the 1924 revision of the American immigration laws went into effect. Under the old law, university graduates and clergymen were in an unrestricted category. The day after Father's arrival, such immigrants were no longer privileged in unlimited numbers. And the annual Hungarian quota of less than nine hundred was oversubscribed for years thereafter.

I suspect that Father had long wished to return to the States. But life before World War I was pleasant enough for him. With marriage and the birth of a child, the time was hardly suitable to pull up stakes. Then the war and Bela Kun's Bolshevik revolution in 1919 immobilized us. During the twenties, when Horthy's Fascists ruled the country in a vain effort to stabilize the economy and society, Father saw the dark clouds on the political horizon for what they were. Losing the war meant stiff reparation payments and ceding valuable lands, rich in raw materials, to the succession states of Rumania, Yugoslavia, and Czechoslovakia. And Father foresaw even more trouble in the future; he proved correct, of course.

Once again, after another world war, Hungary was defeated, again by the Allies. In between there were some relatively comfortable years, but in Hitler's shadow, the Hungarian Arrow-Crossers became a powerful anti-Semitic Fascist group, and they kept the country safely in the master's orbit. Even Horthy wasn't extreme enough for them in the end, and the old Admiral/Head of State was forced into exile. In 1943 the Germans occupied the country. The Russian Army "liberated" it in 1945 from the Nazis and has maintained this "liberation" ever since. What has happened in Hungary since 1933 is what my father managed to avoid for us by leaving it in 1924.

No member of my mother's family had been to America, and they knew no one who had solved a financial or personal dilemma by going there. Father, with or without a job, made a comfortable living and kept us on a standard we were reluctant to give up. After the war, he became a stockbroker and a stamp dealer. Mother opened a couturière salon in our home. She was the designer, and she employed a seamstress to help her with the stitching and sewing. She kept the salon until shortly before she and I left the country in 1927.

We did not accompany Father on his big adventure because we

were not granted our passports in time. Nor did we have American visas. Consequently, it wasn't until three years later that we were reunited in New York.

In the intervening time, I continued my education in the *gymnazium*, where I proved to be an exemplary student. The school was a dozen or so trolley stops away, but I walked the distance many times, partly so as to pick up one or another friend along the way. There were two "best" friends in my life then; until I entered the University of Pittsburgh I carried on a brisk correspondence with one of them.

Outside school, Mother introduced me to the theater and the opera. I was also enrolled in a gym club where I was expected to do physical exercises and learn sports. Ballet I liked. Bars, ladders and rings I was good at, but I found fencing the most enjoyable of all. Twenty-five years later I tried to revive this skill, but it turned out to be an abortive effort. En garde! mesh mask, foils and lunges are but an exciting memory now.

Piano lessons started when I was about eight. I don't remember any of the drudgery usually associated with practice, and I must have been a willing pupil. Mother entertained encouraging notions about my talent; I held the opposite view. Actually, I might have become a competent pianist if I had not given up lessons after high school. After our move to America, I attended special classes for high schoolers at Carnegie Tech (later Carnegie-Mellon University), where Professor Selmar Jansen did his utmost to make me live up to his expectations. With Earl Wild, my fellow student, he succeeded notably. Earl had what I lacked: natural talent, perfect pitch and driving ambition. No wonder he became a prominent popular concert pianist and soloist with symphony orchestras.

Talented or not, at least I developed a feeling for music. In time, I became a devoted listener to good music, much to my parents' delight and my own pleasure. Of our material possessions in Budapest, the baby grand piano was the one piece Mother was most reluctant to leave behind. I suspect that if the piano had been a cimbalom, on which she once was a whiz, she would never have left it behind. A cimbalom is an open-topped stringed instrument played with two felted mallets. No gypsy orchestra can be without one.

My parents taught me how to ice skate. I recall many cold hours on a lake in Budapest's picturesque City Park. There was something very special about this skating facility. In early spring and late autumn, as well as on mild winter days, the ice was maintained artificially through an ingenious web of refrigerating coils. In summer, water sports were available there. Boating on the Danube was not my parents' nor my "thing." But sun and thermal bathing and swimming were. I had a choice among dozens of bathing emporia in the city as well as pools and beaches on Margit Island. In a luxury hotel on the Buda side of the city, there were artificial waves simulating seaside conditions. One of the many wonders of my native city that I rushed to see after thirty-seven years' absence were the waves of St. Gellert, still undulating and still great fun. In the United States, new wave pools are currently being installed. In Pittsburgh, there are already three. A great new invention? For me, strictly déjà vu.

Between the end of the war and 1926, I have some clear recollections of summer holidays. One major social event of my young life occurred in Deva, a small town in Transylvania where, at age eight, I served as junior attendant at the wedding of cousin Olga. I was elegantly outfitted, and I wore a huge taffeta bow in my hair. I also had my first professional manicure for the occasion. There were representatives of all the branches of the Manheim-Stern clan, the large extended family coming from other communities and neighboring countries to attend. But it was the presence of the rich, successful American uncle and aunt and their two older children, Alice and Paul, that made this a very special family party for everyone. Photographs were taken in all possible combinations and of all relationships. Fifty years later I had the unique pleasure of tendering the long and happily wedded couple a lovely golden anniversary party in my Jerusalem home.

I also remember well a journey to Szovata, a mountain resort perched high up in the Carpathian Mountains (Dracula country). The Hungarian, and then the Rumanian, customs officials and border police were uncooperative and downright rude.

Altogether, the combination of senseless delays, lack of refreshments, physical inconveniences and harassment became a nightmare. In any case, being patriotic Hungarians, we had only pejorative words to say about Rumanians at that time (1920 or 1921), the highly cologned and corsetted officers among them not at all helping their image in our eyes. However, our holiday was finally an absolute success. Due to the high saline content of the water, it was impossible to sink in it. And so I learned to swim that summer.

Another outstanding summer holiday of these early years was one in the Semmering mountains in Austria. Cousin Klara was thirteen and boy conscious; I was eleven and just learning to be. We spent a couple of weeks in the charming resort town of Reichenau. Transylvania to me meant mountain hikes, deep salt-water lakes and family visits; Semmering was mountain hikes and picnics, walks and canoe rides in shallow streams. These latter were usually complicated for me and enhanced for Klari (less formal version of the name) by the presence of one of the boys from the hotel who was interested in her and totally ignored me. Another of our pastimes was crouching by the side of the nearby highway identifying different makes of automobiles as they passed. By learning their radiator cap medallions and other distinguishing marks, we mastered the game of auto recognition that summer. I have been a car owner myself for many decades, but today I cannot tell one make from another.

Our experiences with motorcars were otherwise limited. While there were autos and motor taxis in Budapest in the mid-twenties, we most often took a *fiacre* (horse-drawn carriage) as an alternative to the trolley. Once, however, Mother and her sister hired a chauffeur-driven auto so that, accompanied by their daughters, they could relive some of their childhood memories. It was my one and only look at the Fein homestead.

A popular mecca of all vacationers then, as now, was Lake Balaton. The largest lake in continental Europe, it is situated in western Hungary and is surrounded by rolling hills, lush flatlands and picturesque small cities. The shores of the lake itself are dotted with resort towns and villages, each with its own special character. Balaton offers city folk a carefree life of casual socializing, swimming, sunbathing, boating and fishing. Our mothers, Klari and I were there often and for weeks at a time. Our fathers came for weekends or for a short week now and then. Train connections were excellent, and, over the six years that we explored the Balaton, we stayed in several different resorts and nearly always in *pensions*. Several decades later, Harold and I made a trip into my past on the Balaton, driving a rented Hertz car and returning to Budapest by train. Hertz is something new in Communist Hungary; for us, it was a welcome friend from America. For Mr. Hertz himself it was a return to his native country. My cousin Frank Manheim was his investment banker when he was a Lehman Brothers partner in Manhattan.

One particular vacation on the Balaton keeps coming back to me: the summer Mother had my head completely shaved. It was a current fad and I wasn't the only girl thus shorn. I have a photo of me with a shiny bald head, standing on the edge of the lake— certainly not a pretty sight by modern standards. I wonder, though, if there is a correlation between the lavish compliments I receive from hairdressers around the world for the fine quality of my hair and the shaved head I sported one summer on the Balaton!

In those days, two favorite faraway vacation spots for the "in" people were Abbazia on the Adriatic and Ostende on the North Sea. The Monoris and Gabors (Klari) never quite made it there, though my parents had been on an extensive honeymoon abroad. Anyway, we in America more than made up for our earlier lack of foreign travel, but my aunt's and uncle's later major trip was their last, to Auschwitz.

During my first six years, I could hardly have been called a sturdy child: in fact, I appeared to be downright undernourished. I had two major health problems. I was plagued with a rectal malfunction for many months, until an old-fashioned doctor cured me after all else failed. I also almost died from double pneumonia; the crisis occurred upon the family's return from my grandmother's interment, which I could not attend. My body sizzled with a temperature of 41 degrees centigrade (105 degrees

Fahrenheit). Being wrapped in hot, wet, vinegary compresses all through the night was the magic formula used for alleviating the symptoms. This and prayer were the accepted cure before antibiotics.

Not until my summers in Transylvania and on the Balaton was my mother able to enforce a proper diet for me. Gaining weight was the object of the game—the very opposite of my current chronic efforts at reducing. During food shortages (until about 1920), when peasants came into the city with their chickens, geese and produce, it was only the alert and lucky housewife who could provide nourishing food for her family. At one point, Mother bought a gosling with an exciting future as "pet-in-residence" on our fifth-floor balcony for as long as she was willing to feed it. This she knew how to do: corn kernels were stuffed down its throat, fattening it up until it was ready for slaughter. We then had meat, bones, giblets, liver, fat and cracklings for many a meal. This was a highly unorthodox means of feeding one's family in a well-appointed city home. But in addition to being sophisticated, my mother was also practical. The skills and character attributes she learned in her youth in the country served her well in emergencies in later life on two continents.

Only two things stood in the way of our departure for America: a valid Hungarian passport and an American visa. Mother tried every connection and employed every means to induce the Interior Ministry officials to let us go. They didn't see it that way; cutting through red tape took almost three years. There were endless hearings and reams of paper. At the other end, Father had equal trouble in securing prompt processing of our application for immigration. Meanwhile, he sent monthly remittances, providing well for us. Dad's dollars were plentiful enough to allow us to buy new and complete wardrobes, even including a brand new Persian lamb coat for Mother. She wouldn't set foot in the New World without the latest fashions from Budapest, the Paris of Central Europe. Crates of our belongings, including antiques, heirlooms, paintings and furs, went along with us. Opon our arrival in Wilkinsburg, a Pittsburgh suburb, we soon discovered that our new life-style didn't require the use of such fineries. Nor were our material possessions an unmixed blessing in a smoky environment without any household servants.

Finally, all documents and permits were in order. All packing was done, and extra furniture was disposed of. We made our rounds of goodbyes and shed our tears of joy and sadness. Mother was reflective and apprehensive. As for me, the thrill of the ocean voyage and reunion with my father outweighed every other consideration. I was ignorant of America; in geography we had never gotten beyond study of continental Europe. What will be, will be, might have been our motto as we left by Wagon-Lit train from the Eastern Railway Station, with family and a few friends giving us their tearful farewell.

Chapter 3

From Budapest

The finishing touches were barely on the apartments when my parents moved into one on the fifth floor left. This building had been built one year before World War I; we were its first tenants. I was born in it; my four children and husband have seen it. I revisited it fifty years later.

Most Budapesters lived in apartments, though there were those, usually in the upper-middle or upper classes, who owned lovely villas on the Buda side, on woodsy, secluded streets. Number 40 on Visegrady Street was at the intersection of two lovely quiet avenues in a then-new middle-class residential neighborhood in Pest. I remembered the building as elegant, sturdy, and youthful. When I revisited it, I was shocked to see its facing—once smooth, pale beige—bullet-ridden and grey, the house sadly neglected both inside and out. The ornamental accents and architectural details were still attractive, but the lift was decrepit with age and abuse.

I paid a courtesy call on the "housemaster," as we called the concierge, who lived in a two-room apartment in the courtyard. He was astonished that I cared enough to come back and talked of the horrors of World War II, of the Nazi occupation and the siege by the Russians. Then, giving me the key to the lift, he invited me to go up and see my old apartment. As I rode up in the cagelike car, I anticipated every detail. I was determined to see it with my child's eye, exactly as it was when I lived there.

The big hall inside the double-hinged, wrought-iron-framed, solid-wood doors also served as a reception room, light snacks being served there on occasion, and sometimes also doubled as a playroom. It was the hub from which all the other rooms radiated. On the right was a medium-sized room that faced the open-air corridor around the courtyard. It was usually all mine, but now and then part of it became Mother's dressmaking workshop or Father's den. In the middle, opposite the front entrance, was the double doorway to the salon, the largest room in the apartment, which included a dining area.

On the left were a fully outfitted bathroom, a separate W.C. (toilet), and a walk-in pantry, all of these utilitarian rooms having small windows to the outside shaft. Farther left was the maid's room, and beyond that was a modern kitchen—1913 vintage, that is. The bathroom was off a large bedroom, which in turn led into the large salon. Both the bedroom and the salon opened onto one long balcony overlooking the street.

A ceramic tile wood stove, linked to central ducts for fume exhaust, was an important accessory in every room; they were a marvel of engineering and artistry. Natural gas kept the continuous water supply at the proper temperature. The hot-water gas heater, which I remember as a monstrosity, stood in the bathroom. Gas also served us in the kitchen, but the larger kitchen stove was heated with coal or wood. Flatirons were charcoal powered. There were handsomely decorated switch plates for the electric lights, and glittering ceiling chandeliers. The telephone was installed in the hall. Besides its normal function, it provided a most ingenious service of periodic newscasts and theater programming through a central switchboard.

Furniture in Art Deco style, a grand piano, beautiful linens, shining silver and brass, crystal and fine porcelain—objets d' art of all sorts—were the last furnishings I lived with before a more spartan way of life overtook us in America. Art Deco is how we would label the furniture that we then called simply "modern."

Some rooms were wallpapered, some were painted. The salon was decorated with a bold overall design, painted right on the wall with giant stencils. My mind's eye can still see the wreaths of roses against a mauve grey background, because I remember well watching the men with intense fascination while they were applying them to the walls.

The apartment into which I walked after thirty-seven years' absence appeared ordinary and shabby. It was also half its former size, as now two families, good comrades all, shared the space and somewhat updated facilities. One of the tenants kindly showed me around. To me, this was not a middle-class apartment (with upper-middle-class pretentions); it was strictly middle proletarian. Fuss and pretense, not an iota. TV and party literature? Yes, of course! All of it solid, no-nonsense working class.

I stepped onto the balcony. Ahead of me, six blocks away through a maze of TV antennas, I saw the Ferdinand Bridge spanning a wide track bed near the Western Railway Station. Five blocks down to the right, I saw Visegrady Street merge into one of the stately boulevards that encircle the inner city. At that point, were I to walk right, I would be at the Vig Theater, where I had seen Paul Lukas (Lukacs) on stage before his Hollywood success gave him international fame. Here too Ferenc Molnar's plays were presented in the original version in their home theater. If I turned to the left, I would be in the Vig Café, where I was taken by my parents at maidless times and where the literati and journalists settled the issues of the hour.

Did I hear a faint quack of the goose that was our pet one meatless spring so long ago? Did I smell the tantalizing aroma from the bakery shop across the street where we used to have our own homemade bread baked to perfection? The sights, smells and sounds of my childhood transcended the decades. In my mind, all was one. Here on the fifth-floor balcony, suddenly my memories and present reality merged into one. And, once again, Number 40 Visegrady Street was exactly as I remembered it thirty-seven years before.

Between Buda and Pest, in the middle of the Danube, lies the city's sparkling jewel, two square kilometers of antiquities, amusement and romance. The year around, Margit Island is a sportsman's arena, an environmentalist's dream, an archeologist's dig and a giant lovers' lane.

Facing Pest is a promenade for those who walk to be seen and for those who sit on benches watching those who walk. Opposite Buda are a variety of baths and pools fed by sulphur and mineral springs for the alleviation of real and imaginary ailments. Water bubbles up at different levels at different temperatures to cater to the most demanding clientele. A small marina services enthusiasts, while tennis also attracts its devotees. The Grand Hotel (recently remodeled and refurbished) has facilities both for vacationers and for those who only have a few hours to spend. Its restaurant and kiosks scattered elsewhere on the island satisfy the palate and quench the thirst. There is a dazzling profusion of plant life and flowers everywhere. Bus and autos drive in and out; ferry boats also link the island to the mainland. An energetic swimmer can get there in the Danube, as blue as anywhere between Vienna and Belgrade; a pedestrian by a five-minute walk over Margit Bridge. But whatever the means of approach, this extraordinary island gives Budapest a unique distinction among all the beautiful cities of the world.

At the northern end of the island are ruins of ancient Acquincum of Roman times, now the scene of the Budapest Summer Opera. In my day, leaping from one ancient stone to another and games among the ruins were both entertainment and sport for children and romancers.

One activity that stands out in my mind most vividly has to do with the free-style dancing so popular with youngsters of my age. There were always half a dozen or so of us, ages four to nine, who were uninhibited enough to swing and twirl, dance and prance to the rhythm of the band music. We were our own entertainment, and we in turn were added attraction to the adults who listened and watched. Just far enough away not to conflict with the band music were the outdoor café and restaurant of the Grand Hotel. Here were soft music and tea-dancing in the afternoons; gypsy musicians and a dance band alternated in the evenings.

While our parents were enjoying a bit of cosmopolitanism indoors, Klari and I and other children were practicing the latest dance steps outside. "Somebody Loves Me, I Wonder Who?" by George Gershwin (from the George White Scandals of 1924) was the latest hit tune; its lilting melody is still mine on instant recall. The Charleston and the fox trot were the current rage, as were the tango and the perennial waltz.

I've been on Margit Island three times since I left the city; this is one place that not only harmonizes with my recollection of it, but the passage of time actually enhances its beauty and charm.

From what I have said so far about my early years, one may assume that cousin Klari was a significant element of my story. Indeed she was. Our mothers were very close; our parents dear friends. We were brought up as if we were sisters, neither of us having a sibling. We shared common, sometimes intimate, experiences and mutual interests. We were often in each other's company, though we lived at opposite ends of the city. After my departure, we kept in touch all through our teens and young womanhood, until commmunication became impossible on the outbreak of World War II.

My preoccupation with Klari's fate left me no energy to deal with relatives who were part of another parallel drama, that of Israel. This I found difficult and embarrassing—in fact painful— to explain to myself later when I realized how much these relatives and Israel meant to me. However, eventually I learned to accept entanglements of heart and mind as and when they occur. In any case, the Klari story took on a hopeful yet ominous flavor in September, 1945, when finally we received a cable: Married William Ranky—parents Auschwitz—desperately need medicines.

When the World's Fair was to be held in New York in the summer of 1939, we had tried to pressure Klari and her parents to agree to her visiting us in the United States. We planned then to alter her visitor's status to that of an immigrant with whatever legal means might be at our command. Aunt Aranka and Uncle Rudi were against this scheme, and Klari herself did not wish to risk parental disapproval. She had received her medical degree the previous year, and her personal status as well as her professional prospects seemed satisfactory enough. Hitler already in Vienna was perhaps only an idle threat. Why the fuss by the American relatives?

In 1945, when the American army was liberating concentration camps and UNRRA[3] was assisting war victims, I pleaded with friends attached to both forces to find and help Klari. When from the first cable and subsequent letters I learned the ugly facts of life and death she had endured and witnessed, I set myself a goal from which I was not to be deterred. Bringing Klari to the United States was a project that took me three years to complete. While I was the mastermind behind it, my parents and Harold were my teammates. For me, her lot led to a totally engrossing program of action that became an obsession.

My campaign in behalf of Klari and her husband consisted of (1) providing material assistance while they waited, (2) building a legal framework within which they could qualify for entry, and (3) giving material and moral assistance after their arrival, until they could make it on their own—which they soon did with style.

The legal problems were complicated. The Hungarian quota had been oversubscribed for years, and since the end of the war the U.S. Legation in Budapest had been besieged by additional eager applicants. We therefore hired an able immigration lawyer in New York who had an extraordinary record of dealing with impossible cases.

I formulated a plan whereby Klari could enter the United States outside the quota. Our very dear friend and former professor of history at the University of Pittsburgh, Bryn Hovde, was now Chancellor of the New School for Social Research in New York City—popularly known then as the University of Exile. Many eminent scholars from Europe had been invited to join the faculty of this unique institution of higher learning. Bryn agreed to invite Klari to be a lecturer in psychiatry; we on our part contributed $5,000 to the school to cover her salary for 1948–49.

According to the immigration laws then in effect, academic teachers and clergymen—and their wives and minor children— were entitled to nonquota status. However, there was no provision for nonquota admission of a female professor and her dependent husband and children.

The Rankys' case, complicated by the law's absurd use of the male pronoun and *wife* instead of *spouse,* was one I could champion with all my means and a great deal of zeal. I gave the lawyer in New York no peace until he accepted my premise and my logic. Upon my urging, he presented immigration authorities and review boards briefs in which he pointed out the injustice of using the masculine pronoun as the sole determining factor in eligibility. Rosie the Riveter had been a national heroine as well as a practical necessity during the war; and so I now insisted that, in harmony with the times, Klari, the professor, should be allowed to bring *her* husband. I recommended that the rules be interpreted as qualifying the professor and his/her spouse for nonquota admission. Fortunately, besides my semantic preoccupation, the lawyers had several other valid angles and loopholes to work with. And much as I would have relished victory over the Immigration Service on my terms, I was ready to resolve the Ranky case in any way that would legally admit Klari and her husband sooner rather than later. In the end, it was a Cuban visa for him in combination with the New School appointment for her that resulted in their arrival in New York in April, 1948

She sailed on the *Queen Elizabeth I,* just recently released from war duty, and he flew into Idlewild Airport—technically on his way to Cuba—the day before she landed. She never actually taught at the New School, and he never set foot in Cuba. She arrived, however, with rights and privileges of a legal resident eligible in due course to become a citizen. He eventually succeeded in having a special law passed in his behalf according him American citizenship.

While I have been personally involved in many trying situations in behalf of individuals during my lifetime, the Klari story remains my greatest achievement—and emotionally the costliest. What gives me a tremendous satisfaction, even beyond their own success and contentment, is the fact that we have had an exceptionally good and reciprocal relationship all these years. In my adulthood I have in cousin Klari the sister I never had.

Living on Chicago's Gold Coast, Klari is still practicing her profession: with private patients, in the public mental health field, and as assistant professor at the University of Illinois Medical

School. Some years ago, Bill retired from his responsible position in a chemical company; currently his occupation is his lifetime hobby: Henry George-ism. They live well and travel a great deal. They are truly at home in America.

Ferryboats from Pest to Margit Island on the Danube hardly prepared me for a transatlantic ocean liner. In the 1920s one of the smaller ships that sailed between Europe and America, the S.S. *Berlin* of the Nord Deutscher Lloyd, at 15,000 tons was a miniature floating city of lights, life and love. With a passenger capacity of nearly 1,000, she made her maiden voyage in 1925. Though not one of the giants, she was a great passenger ship carrying spinster teachers and middle-aged professors, occasional emigrants, movie stars, diplomats and tycoons back and forth.

I hadn't thought much about the S.S. *Berlin* during the past several decades, though I had clung devotedly to one physical reminder of her, a little silk souvenir handkerchief, hand hemstitched and with a tiny profile of the ship finely embroidered on one of its corners. I had guarded it together with several other delicate handmades, also symbols of a bygone age. But one day, as I sorted and rearranged these and other mementos of former years, I suddenly saw the *Berlin* hankie as a bit shabby and its ecru color an unclear shade of café au lait. And so, in a sudden fit of irresponsibility, I discarded it even as pangs of nostalgia gripped me. After it was beyond retrieval, I repentantly dashed to the Carnegie Public Library to search out available data in connection with my first ocean voyage. Also, an exchange of letters with Lloyd's successor revealed additional information. Being confronted with and now being separated from the little silk hankie finally unleashed memories for so long unspoken.

Leaving Europe on April 21, 1927, from the port of Bremen, Germany, my mother and I traveled in a comfortable tourist (second) class cabin of our own. We embarked with considerable luggage, which included three super crates and a wardrobe trunk bought for the occasion. It stayed in the family through three movings in Wilkinsburg before Goodwill Industries acquired it for the convenience of other transatlantic tourists.

Hoboken does not hold the exalted position Ellis Island has in the annals of United States immigration history. Nevertheless, I am obliged to admit that this is where I set foot on American soil, bypassing Ellis Island altogether. What or whom I can credit or blame for this dubious omission or distinction I do not know. At the time I had no idea either that, defying the stereotype, I was not a part of a pattern millions of immigrants before me had set. A quarter of a century later, when my children questioned me about my arrival in America, I realized how prosaic my story sounded to them, lacking as it did an aura of romance and even authenticity. Although, as far as "romance" was concerned I venture to say that the teeming masses found nothing romantic about the procedures and formalities they encountered on this historic spot.

There was no confusion or haphazard name conferral for us at trip's end. From what I know from subsequent ocean crossings, I can only reconstruct it as normal and uneventful. Exceptions: daily piano practicing in the ballroom and my rite of passage halfway across the Atlantic. In my case, we had our full complement of names and proper documents; we met all regulations imposed by United States customs and immigration authorities. And most important of all, we had my father, a legal resident, as well as his brother, an old-time citizen, awaiting us at the end of the gangplank. At age almost thirteen, I found this the ultimate in happiness.

It was the morning of Saturday, April 30, when we docked at pier six in weather that was a bit cloudy with occasional rain. The temperature on that historic day was in the low fifties, the meteorological reception in no way dampening our spirits.

On that day, in a radio address, Secretary of Commerce Herbert Hoover termed the Mississippi Valley flood "the greatest natural disaster our country has ever known" and called upon the nation to come to the aid of the sufferers. New York City appointed an extra 5,000 police ready for the next day's (May 1) "trouble." At the Yale Club, according to the *New York Times,* H. F. Guggenheim posted $150,000 in prizes in a competition for safe flying: "The idea is to fly people from place to place, not from place to hospital."

We spent several leisurely days with Uncle Armin and his

family in their elegant 1050 Park Avenue home. We did some sight-seeing consisting mostly of viewing skyscrapers, especially the Flatiron Building, which despite its modest height enjoyed considerable publicity abroad. Photographing ourselves with a Kodak Brownie, Father's arrival gift to me, by the Public Library Lion on Fifth Avenue at Forty-Second Street had a significance I could not fathom at the time: it had a sequel thirty-five years later when my daughter—my youngest—was also thirteen. I have a much-cherished photograph of lovely Ellen, a young teenager, on a holiday with me in New York posing in front of the same lion, not at all showing its age or revealing its many secrets. Why not plan a photography session with Ellen and her Emily, my youngest granddaughter, when they are thirty-nine and thirteen, and I seventy-four?

We took a Pullman sleeping compartment on the Iron City Express to Wilkinsburg, two stops before the main Pittsburgh terminal. In those days, even the New York–Chicago express trains picked up and discharged passengers there. After a night or two at the Penn-Lincoln Hotel (now a senior citizens' facility), we moved into our first American home.

Chapter 4

To Becoming An American

If there is a sure formula for learning English other than by being born into it, I don't know of it. But in 1927 I had no choice if I were to make a success of my young life: I had to acquire as best as I could this strange language of Shakespeare and Mark Twain—the only English-language authors with whose works I was familiar at age thirteen (and then only in Hungarian translation). This meant the hard way.

I had arrived in Wilkinsburg three weeks before its school year ended. Therefore I had a three-month period of grace before communication in English became a matter of necessity. Flounder around in the midst of unfamiliar sounds I did! Stutter and mutter I must until September, when the serious work would begin. With a Hungarian-English dictionary in hand, Mother and I faced the rather ungracious world of grocery clerks, landlady, fruit and vegetable vendors, milk and ice deliverymen and an occasional trolley conductor. We discovered quickly that, unless understood, we were laughed at or, worse, ignored.

I was an oddity anyway, with my European cut clothes, and coiffed in two hefty, shoulder-length, dark brown braids. When hot weather burst upon us, I quickly discarded the ankle-high laced shoes that Budapest orthopedists recommended for everyday wear, and I cut my hair to a stylish length. These

additional excuses for ridicule I didn't need. I also changed over
to the crisscross way of handling forks and knives. I found this
way of eating very clumsy, but I considered the compromise a
small price to pay for becoming an American. When I started to
travel abroad, I reverted to my childhood ways, for now the
reasons for the changeover no longer pertained. Eating in the
Continental manner is not any more regarded as a serious
infraction of American rules of conduct. Dangling braids have
also become an accepted hairstyle in recent years for youngsters
and teenagers.

The English language remained as the major impediment in the
way of my Americanization. Fortunately, as I see it now, it didn't
take long for me to find my way in this linguistic maze.

The day after Labor Day, 1927, marked my entry into a
structured environment, Wilkinsburg Junior High School, where
learning English was of the highest priority. The key to survival,
English became a challenge, my purpose and my objective. At
that time, Wilkinsburg had no experience with youngsters with a
language handicap. When Father proposed that I be placed in the
grade appropriate to my age, the principal was kind and naive
enough to agree. Was it wise or irresponsible of her to drop me
into a sea of young teenagers who spoke nothing but English
while I was totally ignorant of it?

And so I was enrolled into the eighth grade and became the talk
of the school system. I was a functional illiterate, but I persevered
in all the subjects that formed the normal program of eighth
graders who had grown up in the English language. That
grammatical and spelling mistakes were constantly part of
students' speech and writing habits proved to be an advantage to
me. It gave me the opportunity to learn rules of grammar and
syntax as well as the intricacies of proper spelling while the other
students were reviewing the same . . . and reviewing . . . and
reviewing. It seemed as if my whole year was spent on basic
English. However, I had also to cope with arithmetic in strange
unmetric concepts and with the mysteries of American history
from the Civil War to World War I. In a few months, encouraged
by my parents and with the help of dedicated teachers and

sympathetic classmates, I pulled my C grades up to Bs and As. In high school, I became an all-A student.

During the previous spring, having said goodbye to school and fellow students of the third *gymnazium* grade, I had had time to read for pleasure. This is how I met Mark Twain. How lucky for me that his *Prince and the Pauper,* which I had read in Hungarian, was on the compulsory book report list. It was difficult enough to write a believable review in my minimal English, but at least I wasn't also obliged to read the book—in English. As it was, keeping up with the class meant, not only after-school homework, but night work. Every night. Total immersion was called for.

Father was the English linguist in the family. Mother learned along with me whenever she was free from her many domestic duties. That first year, she also endured the drudgery of occasional adult English classes at Fifth Avenue High School. This wasn't a happy experience for her; she soon devised more practical and less demanding ways of learning the language. The radio was a great teacher to both of us.

Mastering principal parts of verbs was simply an unavoidable chore. Proper usage of *lay* and *lie* and *let* and *leave* seemed no problem at all; parsing or diagramming sentences became a useful tool and actually a pleasant mental exercise. Finding synonyms, homonyms, and antonyms was an endless search but also a revealing discovery. I probably incurred some antipathy from my fellow students, as the more I liked doing language skills the more proficient I became. But I couldn't care less about their being shown up at a disadvantage.

Spelling caused me much annoyance in the beginning because nothing in English seemed to be written phonetically. (Hungarian is totally phonetic with every letter or diphthong having only one sound.) In spite of this linguistic conspiracy, I made phenomenal progress. Having already had two and one half years of foreign languages abroad, I transferred my acceptance of the unexpected and illogical to English words and to the syntax involved. Father was constantly calling my attention to useful keys to learning English, and I thought then, as I still do, that such crutches are absolutely invaluable. *To, too, two; write, right, rite; letter, later, latter, ladder, lather, leather; lay, laid, laid;* as well as *lie, lay, lain* were games we used to play at home to improve my spelling, pronunciation and understanding of verb forms.

These games paid off handsomely when I started winning first place in the class spelling bees that were weekly occurrences; soon I achieved grade supremacy—over the word *mischievous.* I also learned never to dangle a participle or split an infinitive. In the bicentennial year of George Washington's birth I won honorable mention in a citywide essay contest, under the auspices of the *Sun-Telegraph,* the Hearst daily.

Finally, after just five years in the United States, I was judged to be the second-highest-ranking student in a class of 271. I delivered my commencement address without a mistake or a noticeable accent. The newspapers called this a remarkable accomplishment. I didn't deny the compliment and certainly enjoyed every bit of my scholastic success as well as its attendant nationwide publicity. A clipping service contacted me. Upon payment of a small fee, I received dozens of newspaper and weekend supplement articles about my accomplishments and virtues.

I was deliriously happy over the award of a half scholarship to the University of Pittsburgh as the grand prize for my efforts.

In acclimating to my new environment, I was obliged to face up to one additional handicap besides the language. This was the English system of weights and measures, which seemed to me to be cumbersome, impractical and illogical. How strange it was to make purchases in fractions and measure body temperature and climate in astronomical numbers. Walking so many feet of distance might have made literal sense, but not knowing readily unit prices of anything was quite unnerving. Therefore, besides the dictionary, I carried my little conversion table with me wherever I went.

Moving decimal points was one thing; resolving problems in the odd numbers of the English table of weights and measures was quite another matter. I was distressed to realize that the metric system that I took for granted was all but unknown then by the American public. Pharmacology dealt with it in the laboratory, but nowhere over the counter could one buy anything in grams or meters. I had no choice but to accommodate myself to the nonmetric system. And so, in about a year's time, concepts of distance, weight, volume, and temperature had become clear to me, and I could function in that frame of reference.

When decades later I began to travel abroad, thinking in meters and liters was like meeting old trusted friends again. At the same time, only recently has shopping in England become uncomplicated pleasure for me; the English conversion to a decimal monetary system didn't come any too soon for my convenience. I welcome creeping metrication in America. That in some places distances are already marked by kilometers (as well as miles) and that Coca-cola has switched to liter bottles is encouraging. Equally significant is cigarettes' virtue being extolled by the 120 millimeters—though this doesn't impress me in the least as I am a confirmed nonsmoker.

In 1970 I made a full circle when Harold and I established our home in Jerusalem: weights and measures there are metric. Ironically, I sometimes find myself half-thinking in pounds or inches or Fahrenheit degrees in order to better understand prices or climate.

The summer of 1927 was a transition from the European to the American phase of my life. While I still couldn't read the newspapers or understand radio reports, the Lone Eagle made headlines, and front pages all over the world gave accounts of his transatlantic flight to Paris at the incredible speed of 100 miles per hour. Charles A. Lindbergh was the national hero; Al Jolson appeared in *The Jazz Singer,* a prelude to the talkies. Sacco and Vanzetti were electrocuted, though millions believed them to have been innocent. Will Durant's *The Story of Philosphy* and Sinclair Lewis's *Elmer Gantry* were best-sellers. The Empire State Building was finished, and Ford's Model T auto was new for the last time.

My first impressions of America were of skyscrapers in New York and of smoke and smog in Pittsburgh. Dirt, grime and soot in the Steel City of the twenties were a constant irritant affecting both our health and our way of life. In Wilkinsburg, our first apartment was on a street abutting the elevated railroad track of the Pennsylvania Railroad main line. Even after we moved away from it, the smoke and filth emanating from distant mills and factories affected our homes and our persons. That others similarly suffered did not make the situation any more tolerable. But almost a million people in greater Pittsburgh had learned to live with severe air pollution, and so did we. After smoke control measures were introduced in the mid-forties, we began to breathe more easily. Soon, having to change shirts and blouses at least twice daily and to wash curtains semimonthly were no longer grim reality, merely an unpleasant (dirty) memory.

Father preceded us in Wilkinsburg by three years. Upon arrival in this country for the second time, he spent even less time with his brother and his family than when he was a bachelor. He was anxious to secure suitable employment and to prepare for our joining him. According to his own account, he studied newspaper ads and applied to employment agencies for leads anywhere in the whole country. However, what appealed to him most was an urgent call in bold print announcing openings for mechanical and electrical engineers in the Steel City of Pittsburgh.

The Westinghouse Electric Company was already headquartered there and had its main plant in East Pittsburgh, a working-class community, one of many among nearby mill and factory towns. Heavy electrical machinery, particularly motors and generators, was the company's main product, and switchboard engineering was vital to its development. By the time Father accepted the Westinghouse offer, professional pelple had settled in adjacent residential towns, the largest of them being Wilkinsburg. The schools were good there, and churches stood at every other intersection—a dubious advantage for us. In any case, it was a "nice" town, it had solid middle—class pretensions, and it was as close to the plant as it was to the heart of Pittsburgh. For lack of different advice, Wilkinsburg was where our American life had its start.

Our first apartment was spacious but not very homelike. The long corridor from which all the rooms opened—and on one side only—gave it an institutional air. We were much too close to the tracks; the noise was deafening and the dirt unbearable. We furnished our first American home, not according to our inclination, but rather in keeping with our self-inflicted notions of austerity. Style: Early Immigrant. We bought furniture in second-hand shops and spent endless hours of scrubbing to make it more acceptable. Then, no sooner had we finished outfitting an apartment than we began to upgrade its appearance. Mother gradually discarded one second-hand piece after another and replaced each with new but still undistinguished furniture. Only many years later could my parents indulge her whims and furnish their home in the style that suited both their personality and their station in life.

Were it not for my mother's talent in turning the plainest and most ordinary places and pieces into something cozy and appealing, our three homes in Wilkinsburg would indeed have been drab and depressing. As it was, our living arrangements were not at all bad. I never felt either awkward or embarrassed to bring friends home, even after I crashed through the confines of staid and stodgy Wilkinsburg. In fact, my friends were quite charmed with the ambience that Mother had created. Oil paintings, gleaming silver, exquisite handmades, and several small Oriental rugs, all brought with us from Budapest, made our home stand out among those of neighbors and my girl friends. One piece among all the material possessions we owned in those early years is still with me—a simple curio cabinet that we called a *vitrine*. Mother found it in her favorite second-hand-furniture store on Penn Avenue and paid the grand sum of ten dollars for it. She scrubbed and polished it, and she placed in it some of her treasured antiques to remind her of her Budapest home. I inherited my mother's love of collectibles, and I am pleased to see in my daughter a similar interest.

The neighborhoods where we lived—Jeanette, Mill, and West Streets—were an amalgam of upper working class and lower middle class. Our friends were well educated and professionals. Our neighbors, on the other hand, were a plumber, an odd-jobber, a jewelry salesman, a grade school teacher, a real estate agent, a carpenter, and a retail store clerk. Good people all; uncomplicated but also bigoted and hopelessly provincial. As all of Wilkinsburg was predominantly a middle-class WASP enclave, for us to live in its midst was a novel experience. During those Ku Klux Klan–ish years, most Wilkinsburgers were either ignorant about Negroes, Catholics, Jews and all immigrants or wholly prejudiced against them. We got the message quickly and kept our true identities to ourselves. It was awkward enough not to be able to speak English at all at first, then not fluently—though always correctly—and with a slight accent. But to be known as non-Protestant or even non-Christian seemed to us a greater handicap than we were ready to shoulder at that time. Weak, wise or practical? All of these and none. We were caught up in a traumatic experience. And we were shortsighted. In that place, at that time, because of lack of our own total commitment, we felt no compulsion to analyze our motives. The simple fact was that we didn't know how to cope with this sensitive area of our lives. As for all things, however, passage of time resolved this personal dilemma, and we eventually found our true direction.

Two things about the American public school system I found rather astonishing: an easygoing, informal relationship between teachers and students, and coeducation. I was completely unprepared for either. I was so pleased with the informality that I wrote a long letter of approval to the *New York Times*—but it was never published. Coeducation, however, caused me many moments of embarrassment. In the classroom I had no problems, but outside of it I was a proverbial wallflower. No after-school, walk-home dates, no movies, school affairs, or auto rides with boys for me. Fortunately, I had a number of girl friends with whom I could share activities. The girls all had a "normal" social life, but on rare occasions they had all-girl programs when I too could be one of them. Driving out to the country for hiking or picnicking, suburban public pools, and study sessions were the extent of my social life with my peers. My senior prom —my being a prominent member of the class—was a total disaster. A boy who was a year younger than I and the son of a distant Hungarian-speaking acquaintance of my parents was browbeaten into escorting me. A girl friend of mine was gracious enough to arrange for us to be her and her partner's "double date," but of course I was the first one taken home after the dance. I didn't need much imagination to know why.

During the first five years of my American life, I was as much in the company of my parents' friends as I was among other teenagers. An outstanding example of this was a two-car excursion to Niagara Falls over the 1927 Labor Day weekend. Trips that we took to nearby towns to participate in philatelic shows and sales I recall with no special pleasure. There were also free trips beyond the south hills of Pittsburgh where the air was less polluted, provided by real estate developers using high-pressure methods to lure people to distant sites. Along with private heart-to-heart talks under huge tents, they even provided lunch and band music. Nevertheless, we were well disciplined, and, while we gladly accepted their gracious hospitality, we remained adamant in refusing to buy lots in areas that were so far out, in still uncluttered and unspoiled countryside. Several Sundays were thus spent as guests of fly-by-night entrepreneurs. How shortsighted we were: we failed to foresee trends in real estate values because we couldn't bring ourselves to take risks.

During my high school days, while I wished I had a more attractive social calendar, I thought it was better to do something—anything—than to be an unhappy loner. At most of the adult get-togethers I had some studying to do, and so it was often a case of combining a second-choice engagement with a first-priority duty.

When I became sixteen—in 1930—we acquired an old, beatup 1928-model Chevrolet. Having passed my driver's test on the first try, I became the driver of the family. Father also learned to drive, but he never really felt comfortable behind the wheel. For all the years he had a driver's license, he never became a skilled chauffeur; his total lack of orientation was legendary. We were on our second second-hand car when I was married six years later.

In addition to stamp dealers' meetings, in the tri-state area and as far as Erie, Altoona and Youngstown, we took one major trip by auto: to the Chicago World's Fair in 1932. Here we met several of Father's cousins, one of whom was the widow of M. Joseph

Vago, one of the four architects of the League of Nations Palace in Geneva, where his name still appears.

My parents were rather tolerant about my driving whims. I had the use of the car whenever I wished: for school, to run errands, to go to Carnegie Tech for piano lessons. During my Pitt years, too, the family auto was mine any time I wanted it, much to my and my friends' delight; for mobility, even then, was a great asset.

Trips to New York we made for a change of pace and to get away from the prosaic life in Wilkinsburg. We went by train via Washington, D.C., on the Baltimore and Ohio Railroad. This was much out of the way, and the trip lasted longer than by the Pennsylvania route. But it cost less, only about eight dollars for the round-trip weekend ticket. We thought nothing of sitting up all night twice in order to spend two whole days enjoying the sights and treats of New York and family hospitality on Park Avenue. In those depression years, people sold the return portion of their tickets for three dollars if they expected to stay long in New York. What a bargain either way!

I arrived in the United States at the height of the great post–World War I boom. No sooner did Coolidge choose not to run than Hoover promised two chickens in every pot and at least one car in every garage. Easy-money, fast-profit speculators believed they had discovered the source of eternal wealth. Nevertheless, we began our American life in low key, bordering on the austere. But we did so because of caution and not for lack of income. Father's position at Westinghouse was secure. He in fact received periodic promotions, some in status, some in salary.

And so, when the bubble burst in 1929, we made no significant changes in our life-style. Father held his job right through the depression. Once he was even sent to New York on a special assignment as part of the engineering team that supervised the installation of a ventilation control system in the Holland Tunnel; he had been one of the switchboard engineers behind this project. Even though jobs were eliminated in factories and mills, and engineers and other professionals were dismissed, Father maintained his good standing until his retirement in 1947. He later worked as a consulting engineer, always for Westinghouse, in Baltimore, Palo Alto and Spain, embarking on his last assignment at age seventy-eight.

We did have to compromise for a year and a half during the worst of the depression, when Father was on half salary. During this period, Mother's baking and sewing skills played an important role in maintaining our modest standard of living. I sold her cookies among neighbors and friends. On a half-dozen occasions she worked by the day as a seamstress in homes of affluent folks who might have become our neighbors fifteen years later. She also created her own wardrobe and mine from season to season with ingenuity and a great deal of hard work. We could not have been as well dressed as we were had not my mother altered or redesigned clothes she managed to acquire at clearance sales and in budget departments. Only pride and the lack of proper tools kept her from tampering with shoes.

I recall no deprivation during the depression. In fact, we were periodically bettering ourselves. I have already described the purchase of our first auto. We attended performances in the old Nixon Theater at least once or twice a season; I recall seeing Menuhin in short pants and Paderewski on his own revolving stool. We were frequent and enthusiastic users of the Carnegie Library (free) Lending Department. For light entertainment, we treated ourselves occasionally to a grand movie afternoon or evening. The basic ingredients for this downtown entertainment fare were a film (often a musical) preceded by group singing and followed by a stage extravaganza of name bands and personal appearances by glamorous Hollywood stars. My fleeting second of recall of audience participation in the entertainment is usually punctuated by an image of the little white golf ball bouncing over syllables of the text, which we all sang to the tune of then old-fashioned songs, played on the booming organ.

When I walk into Heinz Hall for the Performing Arts these days, I can hardly believe the aesthetic and substantive transformation. The old Penn Movie Theater's essential architectural features have been restored; and yet, the Penn never looked so dazzling when it was new. Or so I remember. I also recall grand pianos floating about in the flood waters that invaded the Penn in March, 1936.

In the depth of the depression, a highly intellectual and yet extremely entertaining exercise took place which I recall as an outstanding event of my early years in America. It was a public debate between Clarence Darrow and Pittsburgh's Michael Angelo Musmanno, held in Carnegie Music Hall in December, 1932. The subject was "Does Man Live after Death?" and almost two-thousand persons filled the hall to hear these two colorful personalities.

At the time I believed this was the most mind-boggling idea one could possibly deal with. For years afterwards, I read everything I could lay my hands on about Darrow, the famed maverick who starred in the Scopes "Monkey Trial" concerning the teaching of the theory of evolution in public schools. He also defended the Chicago boy-genius "thrill killers," Nathan Leopold and Richard Loeb. Quite apart from the fact that he supported the negative side of the life-after-death question, Darrow became a hero of mine. I had never heard the like of the wit and personal magnetism the two men employed in their debate; arguments and rebuttals, intellect and logic sparked the very air. Both men opened up many doors for me in thinking about abstract ideas as well as public issues.

In the context of the times and in the framework of our own thinking, I had everything I needed or wanted. However, money wasn't to be squandered; it was to cover necessities, some amenities, and intellectual or aesthetic pursuits, and to be saved if possible. The typewriting course my parents insisted on for me was not strictly intellectual, but it proved justified as a means to facilitate my educational goals.

In counting our assets during the depression, my parents would calculate the extent of our means by listing them: so much tied up in the stock market (always a losing battle), so much in the checking account (hovering around $100), so much in insurance policies (private and Westinghouse), and so much in deposits with the gas and electric companies. Father's durable position and

Mother's adaptability were what kept us from despair over the state of the economy.

From the second semester of high school on, my chances of earning a university scholarship seemed excellent. In fact, in the final stretch of the race, I was invincible except for a half point advantage my competitor gained over me in gym and swimming class. Over this half point, I lost the title of valedictorian and slipped technically into second place. The honors, the excitement and the sense of achievement nonetheless were as great as if I had also set a swimming record. The scholarship at Pitt was firmly mine, and that was a colossal financial breakthrough. Half the cost of tuition ($300 a year or $10 a credit) was assured for four years. With my parents also doing their utmost, my college education was thus affordable.

Mother came to America with the idea of amassing a small fortune and returning to Budapest to buy the apartment building in which we lived. As the depression dragged on and part of our small "fortune" was evaporating on Wall Street, Mother fell in love with America. The United States was a wonderful country after all; opportunities at worst were far superior and more abundant than in Hungary. Depression or no, she saw our future irrevocably interlocked with that of America. Regardless of the Japanese engineer who roomed with us one year, regardless of the unpleasant household duties she was obliged to perform, the redeeming features of this country loomed larger and larger in her thinking. By the time she became an American citizen in 1932, she was no longer interested in our returning to Budapest. Though she traveled abroad several times in later life, my mother never actually returned to her native country, even for a brief visit. My husband, Harold, recalls her asking him, "How can I go back to where Hitler and his Hungarian associates destroyed the people of my earlier years?"

Chapter 5

Pitt

The summer of 1932 was notable for many reasons. The Bonus Army of unemployed veterans marched on Washington. The American people were in mourning for the kidnapped Lindbergh baby. The political conventions were nominating Franklin Delano Roosevelt and Herbert Hoover for the presidency. Pearl Buck's *The Good Earth* was on the best-seller list for the second year; Amos 'n' Andy and miniature golf were two of the most popular forms of entertainment in the land.

Times were bad, but for me, this summer provided an opportunity to leave depression concerns behind for a while and spend a glorious vacation at the home of cousin Alice of the New York Manheims. Alice had married Jack Kaplan in 1925, when he was already a millionaire. Cuban sugar was the basis of his wealth. In 1932, when I visited them at their estate at Croton-on-the-Hudson, he was buying up vineyards in upstate New York and taking over the Welch Grape Juice Company. Theirs was a lifestyle as close to upper-class elegance as I could imagine in those days. I met members and friends of the family. I swam in their lake and pools, took tennis lessons from the pro and visited the stables daily. I had the time of my life.

In the fall, I entered Pitt. By 1932 the Cathedral of Learning, the university's forty-two-story schoolhouse, was already in use but not yet completed. I had many classes there during my four years on campus. The lower floors—now housing the famous Nationality Rooms—and several of those higher up were still open to the elements, and most of the building lacked important finishing features. My schedules usually included classes scattered from the Lecture Hall of Carnegie Library in Schenley Park to Alumni Hall on the top of the hill. The ten-minute intervals between classes were always a mad dash from one level of the campus to another, up or down stairways or across green lawns. Frank Lloyd Wright once called the Cathedral the largest keep-off-the-grass sign in academia, which even then we thought was an irreverent comment.

We called our skyscraper school a Cathedral of Yearning. Chancellor John G. Bowman was a controversial figure in our day and stood at the opposite end of the political spectrum from our academic heroes, Dr. Ralph E. Turner and Dr. Bryne J. Hovde. I was one of a group of bright and articulate liberals who were among their disciples. In Wilkinsburg during the 1928 presidential campaign, another student and I were the only ones known to be Al Smith fans. So I entered Pitt ready to vote in campus elections for FDR's New Deal. But I was not yet of voting age. I consequently cast a student ballot for Socialist Norman Thomas out of admiration for the man and his principles. I voted for FDR in the next three elections and remain a Democrat to this day. I see no compelling reason for deserting this political stance, although I occasionally split a ticket in favor of a worthy Republican or Liberal—on the local or state level.

In my freshman year I also joined the Debating Club and became embroiled in a campus battle over Dr. Turner's tenure. However, I never actually performed in formal debates or intercollegiate meets. I was strong on research but remained weak in delivery. My debating meant a great deal to me; I profited much from it; some of my most pleasant extracurricular activities and most rewarding personal relationships grew out of it. Debating accelerated my involvement with Harold, to whom forensics is a natural talent. Debaters formed the nucleus of the school's academically motivated and knowledgeable activists, many of whom later became prominent in politics, law, academia, industry and public life.

Still on the momentum acquired in high school to do my best in my studies I earned exemplary grades. Later, my scholarship left much to be desired. As and Bs were of equal frequency, and frequent Cs appeared to break the monotony. I wrote some excellent term papers (among them one on the organized unemployed), was one of the most active participants in class discussions, and never left assigned work undone. History, economics and sociology were my strong subjects, and the level of my work was commensurate, not only with my interest in the subject, but also with the appeal of the professor. I regret that I never became eligible for honorary scholastic fraternities. I met requirements only for membership in the sophomore and the senior activities sororities.

In one such group, CWENS, I was assigned as "big sister" to a lovely newcomer on campus, a university graduate from Budapest who was enrolled in studies leading to a master's degree in guidance and counselling. There was an age difference between us; she was a senior in the *gymnazium* when I was still a lowly sixth grader. But we were both Hungarian and seemed to have come from nearly similar backgrounds. From an old photo I see that, as her "big sister" and friend, I adjusted her mortarboard cap before she took her place in her class of masters. Auguszta Schutz-Harkanyi and I became fast friends. She was a frequent guest in our home; she sent me several postcards from places of interest on her trip back to Budapest. But I heard no more from her after her return to our native city. Not until a dozen years later did I learn again of her whereabouts. When Edward Teller, the Budapest-born nuclear physicist, became prominent in public affairs and the subject of much review and interview, I discovered that his wife was my "little sister" of our Pitt days.

In Mortar Board, the senior honorary sorority, I learned something about the practical application of the minority representation theory. When we chose our successors, the status of ethnics and Catholic and Jewish girls was one important consideration. I believe we were fair in picking the best representatives of campus activities while bearing in mind the demographic composition of the student body. I appreciated being a member of Mortar Board, and I enjoyed my association with these girls.

Another group of girls on campus, the local chapter of a national social sorority (left nameless to protect them from embarrassment), had a different kind of impact on me. Through campus activities, I got to know one member extremely well, and we became close friends. When she tried to interest me in her sorority, I considered this merely an extension of our friendship. I didn't think much about the implications of membership in an organization that I later learned to be exclusive. I allowed myself to be misled. Flattered and pleased as I was to be invited, I joined an all-Christian sorority. (The Jewish sororities had overlooked me, and not altogether without cause.) When I discovered that membership was limited to Aryans and, at that time, even further restricted to Protestants, I was shocked and overwhelmed by a feeling of shame and guilt. Too late to avoid being inducted, I reluctantly went along with the farce; for, to have refused in the final stage of probation would have caused a scandal. Right or wrong, I considered my own convenience first; I did not feel handicapped by my membership, nor did I think the group lost any of its luster because of it. Although my discomfort was considerable in being trapped in an unsuitable social situation based on deception, I did not have the courage at the time to expose myself. Naiveté and foolishness let me drift along where I did not belong. How different circumstances were when my children attended college from the mid-fifties to the early sixties!

Another important involvement for me was the Inquiry Club, an arm of the YMCA. The club functioned as a discussion group and lecture forum; it was an important instrument for the review of New Deal politics, ills of society and international affairs. It was a perfect outlet for my own interest in public issues and for my organizational energies. I served as club chairman for two years. During the campaign of 1934, I introduced Henry Ellenbogen, a young congressman running for reelection on the Democratic party ticket. His presentation was far more convincing than that of the Republican speaker had been the week before, and he received a tumultuous ovation from the large student audience. Being endorsed by both the Republican and Democratic parties, he was elected in a landslide and was subsequently twice reelected to Congress. Among many important pieces of legislation, the Wagner-Ellenbogen Housing Act carries his name. A prominent jurist in Pittsburgh until his retirement and always a top vote getter for the Democrats, Henry Ellenbogen at seventy-nine has recently completed forty years on the bench, the last fourteen as president judge of Allegheny County. It didn't occur to me then that in a few years' time we would meet socially and that our friendship and that of our families would span more than three decades.

During the summer of 1933, I did volunteer work at the Falk Clinic near the campus. Even as a mere assistant, I felt important and useful; administrative staff, social workers and laboratory technicians found me eager and willing.

During the summer of 1934, I helped organize and was general chairman of a Summer Student Inquiry. Our advertising leaflet asked the question, "Why Not Make Your Summer Count . . . by enrolling in the Student Summer Inquiry?" It promised an introduction to economic and social conditions in Pittsburgh and their bearing on labor, government, relief, leisure time, family life and health. Under the auspices of a voluntary group of high-echelon professionals from various social and educational agencies, the Summer Inquiry delivered on its promise. We had direct contact with living conditions of families and individuals residing in congested areas; we held forums and discussions and took trips to trouble spots. We heard leading personalities in the industrial, political and educational life of the city; we drew up conclusions and considered recommendations. It was a great educational experience for all who participated in it—easily an equivalent of a semester's study in several disciplines. For me, it was also good experience in organization and management techniques.

I shall never forget a course entitled "Social and Economic History of Europe, 1870-1914" given by Dr. Bryn J. Hovde in the fall of 1934. I did some of my best work in this subject. But an even more important feature of this class was a brief incident that occurred one morning early in the semester. A small paper airplane suddenly hit me in the back of the neck. I turned, and a young man three rows behind me grinned. This is how my relationship with Harold began. His version is that he aimed at the pretty blonde beside me; I maintain that he knew full well what he was doing. A chance encounter perhaps, but two years later we were a married couple, and we've been together ever since.

His face and voice were already familiar to me, though our paths had crossed only once before. I first noticed him at an Inquiry Club meeting when he asked provocative questions of one of the speakers. With an accent pure prep-school Virginian and a manner somewhat aggressive, he showed a firm grasp of the legislation under discussion. When I came to the first session of this particular history class, I bargained for nothing more than a good grade for my efforts. I was delighted to see that Harold's aggressiveness also included shooting darts at girls. After we started talking to each other, and then dating, in no time at all I became more than happy that his aim had not been too accurate (as he claimed). As we saw more and more of each other, his drawl was diluted by my Hungarian inflection, and we both ended up speaking perfect Pittsburghese.

With Harold and the group of Turner/Hovde liberals, I began a new collegiate career. The thirties were a perfect setting for the activist, and, if a student was bright—not necessarily an all-A scholar—and cared about his role in society, he had every opportunity to be both visible and audible beyond the campus. In fact, he could, with the support of sympathetic professors, combine his academic work with public activity. We were fortunate to study under such teachers, and we seized at every opportunity to understand public issues and if possible to do something about them.

When hearings on proposed social legislation were held in the State Capitol in Harrisburg, and mass meetings were planned by the unemployed or by WPA workers to demand higher relief allowances—we were there. If bills to be submitted to the House or Senate needed revision, and if publicity was needed to be written for an unpopular cause—we provided it. We helped to plan strategy and to counsel rank and file. I became an expert lobbyist in Harrisburg and a skilled flier writer. For struggling labor unions and for social agencies alleviating our city's ills, we were available for mimeographing, stuffing envelopes, telephoning and chauffeuring. When I reflect on our self-confidence and bravado of over forty years ago, I am astonished and pleased. It was a good fight, and we excelled at it.

Harold was now in his senior year and was making a name for himself in the old AFL craft union in the steel industry. John Gunther, in his *Inside U.S.A.*,[4] quoted Harold as *the* authority on Pittsburgh and steel. From that he went into the inner councils of the Steel Workers' Organizing Committee (SWOC) and its successor, the United Steel Workers of America. After he earned his B.A., he was a full-time volunteer organizer and a leader of the Pennsylvania Security League.[5] During this time, I was completing my last year at Pitt, and I joined him in work for the League. In fact, the summer of 1935 I spent as the executive secretary's full-time but unpaid assistant in the little office that we maintained in Harrisburg. Harold and I collaborated on another level too. For the opportunities available to us at that time and place did not escape us. We also had mobility and ingenuity. In love, and with ideals for a better world, we simply made our own private better world.

To be a student and to be involved both on and off campus didn't require much by way of financial resources. The depression mentality still prevailed, and prices were low. I was on half scholarship, and my parents financed all my other needs and more. I took occasional jobs; for example, I served as waitress for the Shriners and for classy club women. I also earned a meager sum on a National Youth Administration (NYA)[6] project researching for my economics professor, who was writing a book on nineteenth-century England. On my summer job in Harrisburg, I was compensated only for whatever I was obliged to spend on food and transportation, as I spent the nights comfortably settled in the office alcove.

I had no problems except those relating to my personal status. In trying to resolve these, Harold and I indulged in endless talks and cruel confrontations and pursued all possible options. An early marriage seemed alternately a beautiful dream and a hopeless undertaking. And then came the Great Flood in March, 1936. The Ohio and its two tributaries overflowed into factories, homes, theaters, even inundating the point of the Golden Triangle. And so Harold had no choice but to call on me by boat. It seemed now that there was no impediment in the way that we couldn't overcome. On my graduation day in June, our mothers appeared together, and the signal was on to discuss all the practical aspects of our forthcoming marriage. I did not receive a diamond solitaire to signify our nonengagement. Many years later, I could have bought any ring I wanted, but I still prefer to wear the one my mother designed herself out of the two earrings she had as a bride.

Harold began his duties with SWOC, his first paying job. Starting as a field organizer at ten dollars a day, he quickly made a niche for himself in the inner councils of the union itself. After only a few months in the field, he set up a Research Department, of which he became the director, thus also becoming Philip Murray's chief economist. He held this responsible position for ten years.

While he was solving our basic economic problems, I was looking around for a suitable job for myself. I soon found that this was impossible because my future husband was known to fill a very-well-paid ($3,600 per annum) position. Instead, I started doing things that both interested and challenged me.

While I was in high school and our circumstances were modest, my ex-classmates and relatives in Budapest were living well. My excursions were tied to Father's moonlighting (stamp business), and the eight-mile trolley trip to downtown Pittsburgh merely for fun was an extravagance; my friends skied in the Austrian Alps and summered on the Adriatic. We exchanged an old icebox for an electric refrigerator specially priced for Westinghouse employees; their families frequented fine restaurants. My mother struggled with her first wringer washing machine; their mothers kept full-time maids. We delighted in clever household gadgets and labor-saving devices; they reported on café life, balls, corsages and soirées. It is no wonder, then, that my correspondents and I understood each other less and less as the years rolled by. Eventually, our depression and theirs occurred simultaneously, and their personal circumstances began to worsen in other ways as well. By the mid-thirties, they lived in apprehension of darker and darker political/international clouds. We could foretell their future in somewhat surrealistic terms, though the full extent of the tragedy neither we nor anyone else could conceptualize. They were distressed but claimed the unpleasant situation was merely a momentary aberration. In the end, WE and THEY both knew only that they were trapped, and for the time being we were helpless on their behalf.

"WE" and "THEY" came to a sharp focus when I first returned to Budapest. I was emotionally incapable of coping with post-Holocaust matters, especially relating to personalities of my childhood. How I was both a native and a mere tourist and enjoying both I will deal with in a later chapter.

Chapter 6

Marriage

There were not one but two milestones in my life in 1936. In June I earned my B.A. by a comfortable margin but without any particular academic distinction. In September I was married, which in itself was a kind of distinction. We were both twenty-two, and we thought of ourselves as uncommonly mature for our age. We were confident that financially we were viable (an optimistic state of mind) and were hopeful that my in-law problem would resolve itself in time. We were, and it did . . . in time.

My parents were proud and practical. Beyond the minimum that they could provide for me, there was a vast area of desirable possessions appropriate for a newly wedded pair. For the provision of these, they gladly deferred to my cousin Alice who, during the summer previous to the wedding, showed a personal interest in outfitting the bride-to-be. In addition to his many other substantial business involvements, Jack owned Hearn's Department Store, located on Fourteenth Street off Union Square in New York City. Although its clientele was primarily lower middle-class and proletarian, Hearn's carried many solid middle-class brand names in home furnishings and fashions. In addition to providing a trousseau, the Kaplans invited us to spend our honeymoon on their estate at Croton. We could be as sociable or as private as we wished, they assured us. We were only too happy to accept both offers.

Within a month after the wedding, three huge crates arrived at our utterly ordinary apartment, the contents of which could only be described as extraordinary. Complete bedding as well as linens for bathroom, kitchen and dining room, and a generous wardrobe for every occasion! Everything was in excellent taste and of good quality. Alice had canvassed Hearn's for the most suitable items and made personal selections in all pertinent departments. She compiled an extravagant gift the likes of which neither I nor anyone else I ever knew could reasonably anticipate or duplicate.

Except for a period in 1932 when I wore lisle stockings in protest against Japan's aggression in China, silk hosiery was one basic item of my wardrobe of which I never had enough. What unprecedented extravagance to find in this shipment five dozen pairs of fine silk stockings, in two weights and in several shades! After giving away several pairs, I laid the remainder aside in their original wrappings. For the following year or so, I pulled out a pair as and when needed, keeping in mind that my loot was for life. However, I was unaware of the fact that the silkworm's thread has certain properties that render the finished product useless if it is not properly handled. A couple of dozen pairs thus became brittle while they were kept folded and stashed away in the dark recesses of a drawer. They broke into bits and crumbled away after two years. A great loss this was, especially during World War II, when silk hosiery became an extinct species and most of the nylon was used to make parachutes instead of stockings.

We were married at a late morning hour on the twenty-third of September, 1936, in the rabbi's study of the Beth Shalom Congregation on Pittsburgh's Squirrel Hill. The brief and perfunctory ceremony took place in the presence of the immediate members of the two families. By "immediate" I mean the groom, his mother and two brothers, my parents and I. The rabbi, not personally acquainted with any of us, nearly married me to Stanley, my younger brother-in-law. Fortunately, my parents knew their Hebrew names; my own middle name, Naomi, couldn't be more biblical. And so, for the moment it seemed that our being Jewish was not seriously challenged. But this problem nevertheless continued to plague me for years and must also have caused considerable embarrassment to my mother-in-law.

Afterwards, we drove the short distance from Squirrel Hill to Webster Hall in Oakland where the festive wedding breakfast— actually a full-course dinner—took place. This being a weekday, the brothers went on to school and work; the parents and newlyweds retired to my parents' home, where a few of their friends joined us for a round of drinks and a few clicks of the camera. I have in my possession the one and only existing photograph of us to remind me of this momentous occasion.

Harold had a long weekend off from his union responsibilities. We drove east via the old U.S. Route 30—the Pennsylvania Turnpike was still five years from completion—and stopped to visit the recently wedded Joan and Stephen Raushenbushes at their farm near Harrisburg. Thursday night, our first alone and married, we spent in the hotel off the town square in Gettysburg, where Harold's cold blossomed into a full-scale nuisance. Saturday and Sunday we spent honeymooning at the Kaplans', enjoying their fabulous hospitality. They were more than delighted with my choice of a husband, and Harold has been on excellent terms with the Kaplans and Manheims ever since. Between Jack and Harold there was an instant understanding, and Jack predicted an illustrious future for the budding intellectual labor leader. Our honeymoon was an unqualified success.

I never appreciated personal documents until I learned of the difficulties my foreign-born friends and acquaintances had endured for the lack of them. One friend had trouble establishing her voting rights, another was almost not granted a passport. When we came to this country, we brought all our documents (because we had them!), attesting to births, graduations, marriages, and even deaths. Nothing was left to chance—except that we somehow misplaced the original diploma my father had earned from the Royal Technical University of Budapest. Fortunately, in the mid-twenties in the United States, it was not essential to produce evidence in order to be employed as an electrical/mechanical engineer. The state of engineering was then at such a low level that a European engineer needed only to have an air of self-assurance about him, technical knowledge and expertise at the drafting board. My father became an instant success as an American draftsman/engineer.

I shall never know where or how the original document was lost, but, once settled in Wilkinsburg, Mother started official proceedings to replace it. To this day, this illuminated diploma on sheepskin, with its bright red wax seal attached to it with a red/ white/green cord, is one of my proudest possessions. On the back is mounted a notarized statement to the effect that name of graduate had been legally changed from Manheim to Monori and that this diploma had been executed in the current name as per graduate's request. Year of graduation: 1901. Name change: 1904. "New" diploma: 1947.

I have always been an archivist at heart; so being in possession of my family's vital statistics has been reassuring to me. Along with real estate deeds, insurance policies and Israel Bonds, Monori and Ruttenberg safety deposit boxes have always contained birth certificates, Father's *gymnazium* record, marriage certificates and three proofs of United States naturalizations. Both Harold's and my bachelor of arts diplomas hang on a closet wall. The many honorable mentions and statements of academic and other achievements conferred on our children were in my safekeeping until recently, when I decided that the children should be guardians of their own documents.

At the time of my marriage, I insisted on having proof of my own naturalization on a separate Certificate of Derivative Citizenship. Being a minor when Father became a citizen, I automatically achieved this coveted status in 1930. Nevertheless, I deemed a document of my own an absolute necessity. Even in 1936 there was an established procedure for obtaining it, but I gave the Bureau of Immigration and Naturalization no peace until I received mine with my married name alongside my family name. What a fuss I made about the name. Could it be that in 1979 I would be equally concerned if I couldn't have my maiden name on such a document?

From the end of World War II through the late fifties, my

parents and I were continuously involved in sending parcels to someone or other, to one country or another. This we did with humility and a full heart, for we knew the need was great and the requests genuine. The thought never left our minds that, had we remained in Europe and indeed survived the Holocaust, we too would now be in need. We might not always have satisfied our relatives to the last specific detail in the quantity, quality or choice of merchandise, but I can honestly state that we always tried to do our very best.

My familiarity with this subject goes back to the First World War. We were then on the receiving end. Uncle Armin in America did what he could to assist his European relatives, and we were for a while among his beneficiaries. There must have been several parcels sent to us through "Captain Pedlow's Action," as this project was called. It was a well-organized, private, people-to-people program for Americans to help their relatives less fortunate than they.

One parcel from Armin contained Crisco all-vegetable shortening and some tins of pineapple. Mother's disappointment knew no limits. In her culture, anything other than chicken or goose fat was unthinkable (lard was never part of our diet), and pineapple was so exotic a food that we could safely do without it. When mothers and maids stood in queues for pitifully small rations of sugar and flour, what good was it to receive Crisco and "ananas" from America? Truly grateful we were for all the parcels, but alas, we derived no direct benefit from these two items. Crisco did prove to have great barter value, but only later did we learn to enjoy the Hawaiian fruit.

The first request to reach us after World War II was from Klari, now already a doctor for seven years—and it was for medicines. I rushed to our dear friend and family physician for advice. Dr. Leonard Egerman was most sympathetic and responded with utmost generosity. In addition to providing intelligent advice, he emptied his drawers and cleared his table and desk tops of samples. He also opened up some doors to wholesale drug houses and friendly pharmacies. In a matter of days, vials and vitamins, aspirins, antibiotics, sulphas and serums were on their way to

Klari through the United States Military Mission in Budapest, where we luckily happened to have a friend.

Medicines were followed by clothes, flour and other necessities that were either in short supply or totally lacking. The Germans had robbed the country of foodstuffs and livestock. The economy was in shambles. The Red Army was the city's "liberator." For the next year or two, people did without adequate food, clothing, fuel and utilities.

After my first visit to Israel and my reunion with the cousins I had known as a child, parcels were sent to my relatives there. Among them was a supply of antipolio vaccine.

When my children were attending Falk School at the University of Pittsburgh, Dr. Jonas Salk was making his discovery of a vaccine to control polio. In 1953 and 1954, he experimented on selected groups of children at Falk School, among them being his own sons and our two oldest boys, Charles and James. At the time when my young Israeli nieces and nephews needed the precious stuff, it was still a novelty in the States and not yet manufactured or commercially available in Israel. But we managed to secure a supply through Dr. Salk for shipment to Israel. Arrangements were made through El Al, and refrigeration was assured on flight. A cable advised the family of flight number, date and exact time of arrival at Lod Airport. This person-to-person medical shipment was rather an unusual version of an otherwise routine matter. A parcel is a parcel is a parcel. But the Salk vaccine from Pittsburgh to Jerusalem was somehow a very personalized one.

There was a time when Mother, Father, and I were experts in parcel sending. We knew every size and weight limitation. We could fill in forms and customs declarations in our sleep and were *au courant* with every new shortage in the overseas market place. Those were austerity years, and everything I ever sent to relatives in four different countries, especially to the children, was much appreciated. As conditions improved for my overseas relatives, the need gradually lessened. There were other ways I could be helpful. And I was. In any event, parcel sending finally ceased to be a major hobby in my life.

Chapter 7

Steelworkers and War Years

The Roosevelt years provided the perfect backdrop for my developing political and social consciousness. Those were exciting times to be young, eager and idealistic. When recently Harold and I attended the forty-fourth anniversary of the New Deal on March 4, 1977, in the Mayflower Hotel, Washington, D.C., I had a unique occasion to look back on this period of my life with perspective and much pleasure.

The huge dinner party attracted all those men and women who were associated with the New Deal from its earliest days in 1932. There were secretaries, division directors, agency heads, planners and policy makers, as well as some staff persons from FDR's White House. We were the youngest in attendance, most ex–New Dealers being in their seventies and eighties. Some were not well enough to come; some who did attend were tapping their way around the hall with their canes. Many were no longer living. Benjamin V. Cohen, one of the best-known FDR brain trusters, appeared bent with age but spoke with the same youthful spirit that had animated him three to four decades earlier.

For us personally, it was Sen. Hubert H. Humphrey's presence and his un-Humphrey-like brief address that bridged the New Deal era with current political realities so poignantly. We had supported Humphrey in every one of his campaigns over the years

61

and were immensely pleased every time when he remembered well who we were, speaking with us always in personalized terms. Now he had lost his wholesome robustness, looking every bit the cancer-ridden "happy warrior" that he was. Grace Tully, FDR's private secretary, sat by the wall before and after the dinner, holding court; she seemed to enjoy her spotlight. In fact, touched by ripples of nostalgia, we all reveled in the successes of the New Deal.

In those earlier years, Harold and I had pursued New Deal goals as a team; there was no such thing as each of us pursuing independently our own interests. As it was, my interests, both personal and communal, meshed well with Harold's position in the labor movement. There were no career conflicts, and had there been any they would most likely have been resolved in his direction. It was 1936. Among our friends there was one couple whose female half followed a profession distinctly her own, and she has demonstrated great competence and considerable success in her field through the years. But I had no profession; and good jobs and opportunities with a future were scarce. Being a welfare worker did not appeal to me. My contacts in the job market refrained from hiring me because my need was primarily personal, not financial.

Actually, I was not particularly worried. I considered my unofficial connection with the reborn American labor movement and allied liberal causes a unique opportunity for personal growth as well as to make a modest contribution to a better society.

For a brief time, I was active with the Women's International League for Peace and Freedom, founded by Jane Addams. I was even more involved with the organization of a local chapter of the League of Women Shoppers, activists in the field of consumerism. The *Ladies Home Journal* at the time listed it as the largest women's single-purpose organization in the United States, with twenty-four thousand members. Consumers' Union tested, compared and advised on brands; the League investigated labor practices behind the product, lobbied for legislation to correct injustices and picketed when necessary to dramatize an issue. I remember participating on all levels, from writing publicity material and chairing meetings to attending a national convention. I do not, however, recall myself on any picket line, although I certainly had no scruples on this matter. The excitement of meeting with nationally known personalities whose moral support and loan of names Shoppers enjoyed gave my serious undertaking a most pleasant aspect as well. Among them were Lillian Hellman and Tallulah Bankhead; Hellman addressed the Pittsburgh meeting of Shoppers in February, 1939. I fetched her at the train terminal and escorted her around all day.

The 1938–39 theater season in Pittsburgh was an outstanding one. Along with Lynn Fontanne in *Amphytrion,* Ethel Barrymore in *White Oaks,* Gertrude Lawrence in *Susan and God,* there was something new on the stage. A musical revue loaded with social significance, *Pins and Needles,* was the contribution to the world of entertainment of the International Ladies Garment Workers Union (ILGWU). It was a show with a lot of zip and sparkle; music and lyrics were by Harold J. Rome. It had tremendous acceptance everywhere it played. I had a great deal to do with its success in the old Nixon Theater, shouldering responsibilities in promotion, ticket selling and hospitality.

During the three years before my first child was born, I was free to go wherever I wanted. We usually made a pleasant social engagement out of business trips; adding a weekend day or including a dinner at a good restaurant turned any union assignment into a holiday. In all such instances, we kept expense accounts with scrupulous propriety—a habit that prevails to this day. Whether Harold's salary was pegged at $3,600 a year (in 1936) or commensurate with his position of president/chief executive officer/chairman of the board of a substantial industrial enterprise, the principle has been the same.

When Harold was the featured speaker at a union meeting or participated in union-company negotiations, I often traveled with him; the network of cities we visited became the first stage of my "see America" project. Steelworkers and CIO international conventions and special assignments in Washington were also part of my giant geography lesson.

One occasion relating to tight budgets is indelibly impressed in my mind. It had to do with Billy Rose's *Aquacade* featuring Eleanor Holm, the Olympic swimming star who later became his wife. This extravaganza was playing in Cleveland during the summer of 1937, when Harold and I spent much time in Ohio towns where workers were on strike at Republic Steel and Youngstown Sheet and Tube plants. In Cleveland for a strategy meeting with district directors, we desperately wanted to see the *Aquacade*. Unfortunately, we had just enough cash on hand to return to Pittsburgh with a comfortable margin and simply couldn't afford the highest-priced tickets, which were all that were available. I felt cheated. As it was, the closest I ever got to Billy Rose, besides reading about his personal and artistic exploits, was visiting the gardenful of sculptures that he gave to the Israel Museum in Jerusalem, three decades later.

Another experience had to do with acquiring my service of earthenware dishes during these frequent drives to Ohio. Each trip resulted in an additional piece or two and, at end of strike, I had a complete set for eight and some service pieces besides. Factory outlets in southeast Ohio and the West Virginia panhandle were ideal places to stop for rest, refreshment—and shopping.

Never having done much housework or cooking before, I was a novice both in the kitchen and around our first home. This was a dark and dreary three-room apartment on the ground floor, situated in the middle of a used-car-lot neighborhood. From here, any of our future moves could only be "upward" by any scale! I have always thought of housework as simply unavoidable, and one does it or hires someone else to do it. The more ingenuity one employs in doing it, the less one has to complain about. Kitchen efficiency ranks as high in my priorities as office efficiency should in a business enterprise.

One culinary incident I remember well as a minor domestic catastrophe. Harold brought a young man home with him, one who had earlier called on him in his office. Meyer Bernstein was a recent graduate of Cornell University and was preparing to go to Spain to fight for the Loyalists. Before making a final commitment to leave the country, however, he was willing to consider an alternative, and so, in his quest for social and political justice, he came to Pittsburgh and the Steelworkers Union. He probed and questioned; and while we talked, the tender and expensive slices of calves' liver turned tough and chewy. Not realizing that liver needs no more than a brush with fire, I fried it until it had the quality of tanned leather. The dinner lacked flavor, but Meyer listened with rapt attention to our views on the American scene.

That evening, he volunteered his services to work under Harold. In no time at all, he became a well-paid assistant in Harold's Research Department and shortly after was given other responsibilities in the CIO's Washington office. He represented the American labor movement at many international gatherings, and I can only contemplate whether he ever regretted not fighting in the Spanish Civil War. Today, during his retirement years, Spanish society is again in ferment after nearly four decades of Franco—whose rise to power Meyer Bernstein turned his back on over a tasteless liver dinner in my home.

Although the first summer after my marriage was punctuated by violent Little Steel strikes, my next two were more peacful. In 1938 and 1939, upon Harold's recommendation, the union promoted informal summer education programs for its members. I was a full-time, unpaid administrator, for several weeks on both occasions carrying out plans in which Harold and I had collaborated in the first place. Each program of studies consisted of lectures about labor union history, social legislation, lobbying and current events. The setting was quite primitive, though pleasant enough. One summer course was given in Camp Davis, a former Civilian Conservation Corps (CCC)[7] camp near Cumberland, Maryland. The other took place in the recently developed recreation area Racoon Creek Park, twenty-five miles west of Pittsburgh.

It was great fun organizing classes and securing speakers and literature for our budding labor leaders in the steel industry. I also planned entertainment but left sports to those more competent to deal with them. One of the young students was I. W. Abel, a local union officer from Canton, Ohio. In 1977 he retired from the presidency of the Steelworkers after serving for twelve years.

Robert R. R. Brooks, professor of economics at Williams College, spent about a week with us gathering information about the union for his book *As Steel Goes*[8]—and inscribed a copy for us as follows: "To Harold and Kitty with affection and appreciation of the very great aid which they contributed to the completion of this book." Dr. Boris Stern, an outstanding labor economist and for many years in the Bureau of Labor Statistics, also spent part of his vacation with us and our students. We saw a great deal of each other during our Washington days, and we have kept up our contact to the present.

A charming and bright young Wells College graduate, eager to lend a hand, became my assistant. A daughter of Harold's family doctor, just a couple of years younger than we were, she wished "to do something meaningful" while making up her mind about her future career. We knew her again in the late forties and know her still as Judge Marion Finkelhor of the Court of Common Pleas of Allegheny County.

Between 1938 and 1941, Harold was a frequent lecturer in the Harvard Business School. Although I never attended his lectures, I knew that I had every reason to be proud of him. An academic engagement was high on my prestige list. At that time, I hoped he would develop this area of his activities. While this hope didn't quite materialize, as time went on, I continued to be proud of him for his scholarship, as demonstrated in his writings and in his public speaking engagements.

During the spring and summer of 1939, another couple and we shared a weekend cottage in the Laurel Mountains twenty-five miles from Pittsburgh. By my present standards, I would call it a shack, but then we were oblivious to the physical inconveniences. There were endless discussions with friends about Nazi supremacy in Germany, its likely consequences in the United States and the fate of the Jews. We were also able to listen on the radio to Hitler's mad ravings, with reports and commentaries by Elmer Davis and Raymond Graham Swing.

War in Europe seemed inevitable, and I felt moments of depression. The Europe I had left behind a dozen years earlier was very real to me; I still felt a personal connection with it.

In spite of my occasional preoccupation with the possibility of war and destruction—how devastating it would be I could not know—the coming of my firstborn was a special joy. I was in excellent health and under sympathetic medical care. Harold and the parents were thrilled at the prospects, as was I. Charlie could not have been born under more favorable circumstances—nor could Jimmie, Eddie, or Ellie. To anyone doubting our planned parenthood scheme, I can only cite the birthdays of the boys, all within a fifteen day span in November. Daughter's birthday in June can be rationalized with confirmation (at sweet sixteen) and graduation dates. The children's marriages all occurred in August, although I had virtually nothing to do with the setting of those dates. For childbearing I did, however, have a specific timetable: a ten-year plan for four, from my twenty-fifth to my thirty-fifth years.

The reception following the marriage of a college friend was held on the first Sunday evening in November. Heavy and clumsy as I was, I danced practically every number, and in fact I think I was on my feet all evening showing off. The next day I was understandably tired, and that night Harold rushed me to the hospital with obvious signals of the impending birth. Charlie's arrival in 1939 was my compensation for not being able to vote in that day's local elections. Those were the days when a ten-day to two-week lying-in period was routine. I had the maximum arrangement all four times, and in no way do I apologize for it.

Harold's work was on many levels: speaking on platforms and from soapboxes, directing picket line strategy, negotiating labor contracts, testifying on pending legislation before congressional committees. He wrote and spoke both for himself and for the union. Behind every written or oral statement were countless hours of research and analysis for which he was responsible as Research Director. Harold was a brain truster under John L. Lewis, Philip Murray and Clinton Golden.

One of the architects of the newly formed labor movement and especially of the Steelworkers' Union, Golden was the one who saw the need for a strong Research Department and recognized Harold at age twenty-two as the most suited to fill this position. Harold and I became close friends with both Golden and his wife, Dora. This warm relationship was maintained in, out of and after the union. On an occasion when the Goldens were obliged to leave their daughter behind while attending an important union function out of town, Olive stayed with us. She was as bright as she was a challenge; and at age twenty-three, I liked being considered mature enough to look after a twelve-year-old girl for a week.

In one instance, Harold's admiration for Golden went beyond reasonable limits, so I thought. *The Dynamics of Industrial Democracy,* published by Harper & Brothers in 1942, was an intellectual and literary effort that Harold himself executed. The research behind it, the coordination it required, all of the writing, and dealings with the publishers were all Harold's doing. In many minor but nonetheless essential ways, I collaborated. As I saw it, Golden's role was that of a person whose encouragement and inspiration made Harold's involvement possible in the first place. Harold, however, felt great respect for the older man, and to demonstrate this, he insisted on publishing the *Dynamics* under joint authorship. Not only was Harold not satisfied to give Golden credit and honor with a suitable dedication and some fitting references, but he had Golden's name listed first. *Dynamics* received much professional acclaim and became a phenomenal success down through the years. A classic in its field, it was translated into German, Italian and Japanese, and became required reading for nearly all college courses in labor relations across the country. In 1973 Carpo Press reissued it in hardback.

Harold and I were pregnant at the same time, he with the book and I with our second child; we were successfully delivered of both. To keep in step with my burden, pleasant though it was,

Harold had the hectic last weeks of additions, deletions and corrections to deal with in addition to his twelve-hour working days. Pressures from Harper & Brothers and the need for checking out facts and refining phrases were mounting. Therefore, with my mother's assistance, we went to stay at a farm near Somerset, Pennsylvania, where accommodations for paying guests were excellent and for our two-year-old toddler most suitable. Mother's presence was invaluable, as I was busy with some technical chores and in typing the last draft of the *Dynamics*.

Another of our friends was an able lawyer, Lee Pressman, chief counsel of the Steelworkers and close associate of John L. Lewis. A controversial character, Pressman was a product of Hester Street of the Lower East Side of New York City and a graduate of Harvard Law School. Harold had countless conferences and discussions with Lee, in which I often participated. An easygoing camaraderie prevailed between us for many years, even though Pressman's basic philosophy differed so much from ours that we could never be personally very close. But in those days of Soviet-American Friendship, his adherence to the Communist party line was no impediment to his great service to the union. Lee was a tough adversary and constantly in the headlines. He had great charm and was a stimulating conversationalist. A few years after his departure from the union, he died in relative obscurity.

All the areas of Harold's activity were fertile ground for communing with other bright minds, persons highly motivated and thoroughly competent in their fields of specialty. Both because I entertained New Deal associates at home and because I was able to attend meetings and talkfests, I knew well everyone whose path crossed Harold's.

There were many men and women prominent in public life whose company and friendship we enjoyed in those early years of our married life. In journalism, in government service, and in the liberal professions, there were those who needed to know the pulse of this new force in America, the CIO. Holding a key position in the Steelworkers leadership and indirectly in the CIO, Harold was an obvious target for interviews. He became an invaluable source of information on the objectives and philosophy of the union. Louis Stark, veteran labor reporter of the *New York Times;* other articulate observers of the American scene, such as Russell W. "Mitch" Davenport of *Fortune* magazine; and author John Gunther were among those at one time or another in close personal connection with us. So were government agency heads and especially fellow economists Leon Keyserling and Robert Nathan, with whom our relationship continued past our union days to the present.

One young WPA[9] artist whose signature today commands a six-figure amount did the illustrations for our union brochures and booklets. In 1967, when we were already serious art collectors, Harold discovered an original drawing by the WPA artist among his union papers. Wishing to authenticate Ben Shahn's drawing, we took it to his New York gallery, run by the late Edith Halpert, and asked an associate of hers to give the drawing to Shahn for his signature. In a phone conversation with him at his home in Roosevelt, New Jersey, he assured us that he would gladly sign it and add a reminiscent note as well. Later when we called at Halpert's for our Shahn memento, we were informed that it had been misplaced. It stayed misplaced until after Shahn's death, when we realized that we shall never be able to retrieve it. However, we later acquired a beautiful Ben Shahn silkscreen, a blue, gold-accented Menorah, of which there are only three. He later reduced it into a lithograph for his famous Haggadah, and the design has also been made into a magnificent tapestry. In the late 1930s, when we and Shahn spent many hours together in dozens of sessions composing union literature, he was developing his social realism philosophy. He continued to express his feelings against tyranny, injustice and poverty even as he moved closer, in his later years, to biblical and Jewish themes, subjects that always had a great attraction for him.

There were trips to strike locations, to meetings, conventions and college seminars, as well as visits in Washington. In 1946, I attended a union convention in Atlantic City to which we took our two sons, then aged six and a half and four and a half. I was also pregnant with the third boy. This was our last formal connection with the union, for by then Harold had decided to embark on a new career. Together through the war, the union and Harold in 1946 were at the crossroads of new directions. And so they parted—as friends. There was a touch of sadness in the parting, but we struck out for ourselves with high expectations. And with great inner satisfaction with the role we had played for ten years, we moved on.

In 1942 we bought a three-story house on a three-block street in Pittsburgh. There were four bedrooms on the second floor. Shortly after moving in, we installed a genial bachelor on the third. He paid us very little rent and was practically invisible, but his skill in restoring leaky faucets and faulty wiring was phenomenal. We lived in this house in two installments: until we moved to Washington for government service in 1943, and after we returned to Pittsburgh in 1945, shortly before Hiroshima. I recall this lovely Solway Street property for its only bathroom for two floors, its very old-fashioned kitchen, its interesting fireplaces, and an exquisite Bohemian crystal chandelier in the music room. At this time, we already had an upright piano, and I was taking piano lessons again after a ten-year interval.

It was at this time that I met Marcia Davenport. Here was a woman with an illustrious background, enormous charm and limitless talent. Daughter of opera diva Alma Gluck, wife of *Fortune* magazine editor Russell W. Davenport and stepdaughter of violinist Efrem Zimbalist, Marcia lived an exciting life and had always been surrounded by outstanding people. She was a prominent personality in the world of arts and letters in her own right. Her book on Mozart was already a classic, her *Lena Geyer* was a notable achievement, and her *Valley of Decision* was then being published by Scribner (1942).

As to how we met in the first place, I can only admit what with few notable exceptions has been the pattern all along—that she was Harold's friend. Russell Davenport had interviewed Harold for *Fortune* articles on the steel industry and on the economy in general; and he had been in friendly connection with us since then. He wrote a warm introduction to the *Dynamics* in 1941. On one of our visits in New York, Mitch and Marcia made a social occasion out of our presence, and from that moment on Harold became Marcia's resource person on the steel industry and steel towns for her *Valley of Decision*. In the copy of this volume that she sent us, she wrote, "In great appreciation and admiration and with thanks for the generous help without which I could not have written this book."

Marcia, in her research, made many trips to Pittsburgh, thus providing innumerable opportunities for us to get to know one another. Because of the novel's setting, the publication of *Valley of Decision* was an exciting literary event in Pittsburgh. As the author of this nationwide success—on the best-seller list for fourteen consecutive weeks and later made into a film—she was wined and dined by the social and literary establishments. She invited me to attend many of the special events held in her honor, one of which took place at the Twentieth Century Club. I got devilish pleasure out of being an honored guest at the place where I had once worked as student-waitress. Neither Marcia nor I paid any attention to the fact that, except for this uncommon circumstance, neither she nor I would have been eligible for membership in this very chic and exclusive club.

We also gave a party for Marcia in our own home in order to enable her to meet our friends: Labor Board officials, newspaper editors, persons active in liberal causes, doctors, lawyers, dentists—and musicians from the Pittsburgh Symphony. My parents were on hand to keep an eye on the children, who kept running downstairs way past their bedtime. I didn't know it then, but it was this affair that launched me as a hostess, a role I have enjoyed ever since. Carl Voss, who was one of the guests, reminded me of it some thirty-two years later. Not all my parties of later years had a dynamic personality like Marcia Davenport as a focal point, but, having learned from the success of this one, I continued to entertain celebrities in a variety of fields as and when the opportunity presented itself.

There was one guest whom Marcia herself requested. He had been a musicologist and conductor in Vienna and Berlin before World War II and was then in Pittsburgh. Having been brought to the United States only four years earlier by Eugene Ormandy, Dr. Frederick Dorian was then professor in the Music Department of Carnegie Tech. Prominent in music circles, an author of several books, he has also written the program notes for the Pittsburgh Symphony for over three decades. His latest honor was a coveted invitation to be the guest of the city of Jerusalem for three months in 1978, in the realization of which I had a crucial role to play.

At about the time the World War II draft would have caught up with Harold, he was suddenly affected by a new regulation that exempted men over thirty with two children. Philip Murray also stressed his need for Harold in the war effort. The War Production Board had been set up to deal with the allocation of basic war matériel, and Harold was the union's choice for the post of Assistant Director of the Steel Division. This position turned out to be a significant one and for us both was a reasonable alternative to serving with a uniform on, commissioned officer or Plain GI. Harold's old antagonists in the steel industry suddenly became his associates, and, outside of the combative framework of labor-union negotiations, he came to know some of them personally. We continued a friendly relationship with these associates for many years after the war. Even today, a former War Production Board buddy turns up now and then in Harold's business life. Postwar reunions of the WPB hierarchy, which we periodically attend, have been held in the sumptuous setting of the Greenbrier in White Sulphur Springs, West Virginia—a vivid outward symbol of the change that has taken place in my life since the ex–CCC Camp Davis days of the union.

On the whole, the war years in Pittsburgh, both before and after Washington, were rather uneventful. Occasional attendance at the theater and concerts was the only outstanding distraction in our daily lives. We sold our Oldsmobile to conserve gasoline. Tin cans were flattened after use, and clean newspapers and magazines were saved for recycling. Meat and butter were rationed; I stood in queues for purchase of nylon stockings. Civil defense measures were in effect, and black curtains and blinds became the vogue in household decor. In observing blackouts, my task was made easy by our particular floor plan. During an alert, we simply convened in the second-floor center hall, from which the only light escape was through the stairway window. This was covered with regulation black cloth. We were quite comfortable in this tiny area on the several occasions we retreated into it. For there was room for the crib, space on the floor for play and for chairs, and electrical outlets for lamps and other necessities. Most appreciated of all was the convenience of running water and plumbing in the adjacent bathroom. This was the worst of our civilian "sacrifices."

Dorothy Thompson and Walter Lippman were the outstanding opinion makers in the press. Edward R. Murrow, Gabriel Heatter and Franklin Delano Roosevelt on radio informed, angered or entranced the general public. Generals Bradley, Patton and Eisenhower were winning the war on the battlefields. But for us, in this third term of FDR, our country's capital was the hub from which radiated history-making decisions and directions. To hear the heartbeat of the American war effort, both military and civilian, and to feel the swirl of visiting Allied delegations and dignitaries, Washington, D.C., was the place to be in 1943 and 1944.

Our tour of duty in Washington consisted of exceedingly humid summers, constant visitors, and a livelier social life than ever before. Air conditioning was in its infancy; few government buildings were as yet so climatized. At our house in Silver Spring, Maryland, with the help of an occasional day worker, I carried mattresses and the pillows of overstuffed sofas and chairs outside for proper airing in an effort to keep us all from mildewing. Another household chore, much pleasanter, was carrying the weekly wash to the laundry four blocks away. There was no sidewalk, and I don't remember how I managed this as, with one hand, I wheeled the little one in the stroller and with another I held the older boy. That was the time and place when I could have used a shopping cart, a great technological achievement just coming on the market and with which Harold and I became intimately associated twenty years later.

My parents and my mother-in-law often came to visit us in Washington. They were always welcome, and they never doubted it. This was the first time that we had lived away from our parents and, while the Monoris always had a home of their own, my mother-in-law, at this period of her life, did not. During the years when she divided her time among her children, I never knew when a visit might become an actual living-in arrangement. Because of a natural reluctance on my part to spell out our house rules, privileges and obligations, there were in Washington—as in Pittsburgh—minor disagreements between us. But they must have been minor indeed, for we continued to live side by side, occasionally even together, in wholesome harmony. Apart from the normal personality differences between us, in the seventeen years that we were an in-law pair, we enjoyed a bond of friendship, mutual respect, and benevolent tolerance for each other's differences. In fact, we were quite fond of one another. I was always conscious of her positive attributes, even though I felt from time to time that she dealt harshly with me. But as she was my husband's beloved mother, I had no choice but to overlook certain unpleasantnesses and to accentuate the positive in our relationship.

While we lived in Washington, my younger brother-in-law Stanley served in the Quartermaster's Corps and was stationed at Fort Meyers, Virginia. Through Harold's good offices, he was accepted in an officers' training school shortly after induction. As a dashing young lieutenant, he used to appear in our home between assignments; once or twice his wife, Gertrude, joined him from Pittsburgh for a brief holiday. Stanley was no stranger as a houseguest, having lived with us when we were still newlyweds. There has been an easygoing friendship between us ever since the few months of the winter of 1936–37, when we lived in my mother-in-law's home in fashionable Mount Lebanon, a Pittsburgh suburb.

Stanley was then in his last semester before graduation from the University of Pittsburgh and had a great deal of written work to complete. He didn't mind deferring to me in matters of spelling, grammar and sometimes even of style. And so I helped him with his compositions and term papers. A year later, he lived with us in our one-bedroom apartment while Harold was busy trying to place him in a suitable position. I made a home for him and assisted in his social life. The girl I picked for him, Harold's secretary in the Steelworkers' office, is the girl he also chose for himself, as his wife. Gertrude and he were married in 1940.

After considerable effort, Harold succeeded in providing the right opening for Stanley. Thus he started his working career as a union field organizer for the Steelworkers. He later became a resident assistant to Charlotte Carr at Hull House in Chicago. Harold coached his younger brother in the art and practice of being a labor economist, and Stanley was a good student. He became Research Director of the CIO and filled this position ably until his appointment as Assistant Secretary of Labor in the Johnson Administration. He is now head of his own consulting firm.

Brother Milton was also lucky in his profession. A graduate of the University of Pittsburgh School of Business Administration, he held a drab, low-status job in the late 1930s as accountant for a produce firm. In 1942, through Harold's friendly connection with the Rockwells, Milton secured a more suitable position as an accountant in their large automotive parts plant in St. Louis (now converted to armor plate production)—and in deferment from army service. Milton rose steadily in responsibility and after years of service retired at the age of sixty-three. Milton married Mollie shortly after our own wedding. He died in 1978.

It was during our Washington days that the relationship between Harold and Col. Willard E. Rockwell ripened into friendship. They had first met in 1936 when Harold was on a picket line during a labor dispute between the union and the Standard Steel Spring Company in Coraopolis, Ohio. Harold let the head of the company through the picket line, and the older man took a shine to the young labor intellectual. For over forty years, the Colonel has shown a special liking for Harold and me, including us in many special family celebrations in recent years and extending to us small personal courtesies, as well as substantial help in business. A 1909 graduate of MIT, he pioneered in truck-axle development, and his enterprises eventually grew into Rockwell International. He was such a dear that, many years later, he was a sponsor for a pleasant undertaking I was involved in. I arranged for the MIT Concert Band, in which Jimmie played first trumpet, to perform in the Pittsburgh Y music series in 1963. The Colonel not only allowed his name to be used, but entertained the band privately.

Steve Raushenbush, our friend from the Pennsylvania Security League "unemployed" days of the mid-thirties, was also in Washington. He had been a public power expert in the Interior Department when Harold Ickes was its head; while we were in Washington, he was with the Board of Economic Warfare. We often visited to talk things over and to "pick each other's brains." Steven, now in his eighties, and Joan live in Florida, where we have also visited them several times.

Arthur Goldberg, when we first met him, was a major in the Office of Strategic Services; we had occasional contacts with him during our service in Washington. Harold later prevailed upon Phil Murray to let Goldberg replace Pressman in the CIO; Arthur served the labor movement as Chief Counsel with distinction during the middle and late 1940s. At the time we knew him best, our last and his first year in the union, Arthur's greatest prestige in public life was still ahead of him. His predecessor's career had peaked in the union. But Arthur, never having been burdened by a personal link with the Communist party, as was Lee, continued to distinguish himself in the law and in the public arena. After his term with the CIO, he became an outstanding public servant as Secretary of Labor, Justice of the Supreme Court, and eventually as United States Ambassador to the United Nations. He continues to make important contributions to the fields of human rights and Jewish affairs.

Our dollar-a-year status gave me much pride and satisfaction. The job, the symbolic fee attached to it and the opportunities it provided both of us made the war years in the capital a very special period in my life. Two checks—for eighty-two cents and fifty-eight cents—signed by the Treasurer of the United States and appropriately framed, recall it vividly. In 1944, when Harold had achieved his immediate objectives in the areas of productivity and steel allocations, we returned to Pittsburgh, to the

Steelworkers and to the house we had rented to an army psychiatrist during our absence.

Our oldest child was born when we were exploring back-to-nature country living in a four-room cabin on a chicken farm on the outskirts of Pittsburgh. The second child appeared in our midst in a spacious but oldish three-bedroom apartment. Our third child was born when we lived in a four-bedroom house of our own. In my admiration for the late FDR, I gave the unsuspecting baby Franklin as his middle name. I did not divine then that later disenchantment in FDR's policies with respect to the Jews of Europe would have precluded such a move. The older boys were now seven and five, and with the new blonde-ringleted baby I had an enviable trio of children. A major move to a new way of life however, confirmed our basic desire to complete the family plan Harold and I had set for ourselves earlier. We were hoping that our fourth and last child would be a girl.

Chapter 8

Leaving Labor

Friends were surprised that the transition from the "labor side" to the "company side" was smooth and uncomplicated. Some of our associates called our move a betrayal; others were plainly envious. All of them wished us well. Philip Murray wrote in a warm and reluctant acceptance of Harold's resignation, "I am hopeful that your new associations will provide opportunity for you to build on those fine constructive labor-management relations that ought to prevail in American industry." We thought of ourselves as merely taking a step in another but not a contrary direction.

In 1945 Harold's union salary was $10,000 a year, at that time considered to be within a high income bracket for professionals. As Vice-President of Portsmouth Steel Corporation, he earned $40,000 annually plus stock options, which clearly placed us in a much higher economic category. We both acted immediately in response to this new situation. He tripled his insurance coverage, and I made some adaptations in our outward appearances, which I thought to be highly desirable. Nothing reckless, just a bit of loosening of normal restraints. I now bought better clothes for myself and the children and opened charge accounts at Saks Fifth Avenue and Best's in New York City. (The latter no longer exists, having been replaced by Olympic's monumental glass box

skyscraper.) At this time of my young life, an easily manageable
domestic organization and an attractive home were high on my
priority list. So, for our new home in Portsmouth, Ohio, we
bought every automatic laundry and kitchen appliance then
available and ordered custom-made drapes in coordination with
wallpapers, carpeting and upholstery. To achieve these outward
symbols of material well-being was most reassuring. Many other
options, such as trips and camps, and substantial gifts now
became possible without financial strain.

Our new house was large and included the latest in kitchen
design. More than that, it was exclusively situated on the top of
Timlin Hill with an expansive view of the town below us and of
the Kentucky hills across the Ohio River. The only other resident
on our hill was Pauline Taylor, who lived in an English
Tudor–style mansion with a staff of servants. She was the wealthy
widow of Harry E. Taylor, former owner of the region's
newspaper chain. A septuagenarian, she took to us at once and
even allowed the children to run about in her formal gardens. She
liked me so much that at times her invitations for tea and chats
about art, music and books became a bit of a burden—although I
was of course flattered by her attentions. By virtue of Harold's
position in the company, we suddenly became leading citizens,
especially in the Jewish community. We were fresh young talent
and just what Portsmouth needed, we were told.

It was quite obvious to me that I was expected to be a pacesetter
among my fellow Jews and to become a patron of the arts in the
general community. Even with looking after husband, home and
three active youngsters—not necessarily in that order—I was both
ready to meet the challenge and anxious to do well at it. My
previous hostessing had been mostly personal in nature, but in my
present position a tea or a meeting in my home was regarded as a
guarantee of success in a fund-raising drive or community
project. We had wonderful friends, both Jewish and non-Jewish.
Thus twenty-one months went by in a most pleasant manner.
Happily engaged in child rearing and hostessing, I also became
an active member of a synagogue, the B'nai Avraham (Reform)
Temple—my first affiliation with organized Jewry. The children

were enrolled in its religious school—their first conscious contact with their Jewish identity. The Jewish Community of Portsmouth numbered about fifty families, many of whom were in the legal or medical professions or owned retail stores. The temple had been established many decades before through the generosity of the Richman (clothing) family, who originated in Portsmouth.

Every important Jewish organization had branches in this community. Most members of one were members of all, and some served as leaders simultaneously in all the organizations. If ten Jews met together, it could have been for the temple, or Hadasssah, or B'nai B'rith, or the United Jewish Appeal, depending on the need of the hour. I credit Portsmouth with the first stage of my education in the work of organized Jewry.

Not counting the scholarly rabbi-teacher of my childhood who taught me for two hours a week throughout the school year—here is where I met my first "real" rabbi. Eugene Mihaly was a seminary student from the Hebrew Union College who spent his weekends attending to all the religious needs of our community as a practical application of his studies. Harold had already heard of Eugene, having been asked by his father-in-law, Eugene Bramer (President of Copperweld Company), to find a suitable apartment for him and his family in Cincinnati. (There was an acute housing shortage across the country at this time.) This Harold was able to do through his Cincinnati sales office. Now we were indeed pleased to welcome Gene to Portsmouth and even happier to receive him in our home for the Passover Seder. This is how I was reintroduced to the beautiful ceremonial of this festival meal which I could only vaguely recall from my childhood. In fact, I remember myself as being rather casual about holiday observances, though gastronomic delights associated with Jewish holidays were always featured in our household.

Eugene Mihaly, from an Hungarian orthodox background, had come to America as a youngster; he was now studying for ordination as a Reform rabbi. We admired this young rabbi-to-be for his knowledge and enthusiasm. I never expected to see him again after Portsmouth, but through quite improbable and unforeseen circumstances, we met again in Cincinnati twenty-one years later, when he was one of the favorite professors of our rabbinical student son, Eddie, at Hebrew Union College. Another professor at HUC, Dr. Alexander Guttman, under whom Eddie did his doctorate, became his close friend and mentor. We, too, enjoy an ongoing friendship with Alex and his wife, Manya.

We made several trips out of Portsmouth on business, pleasure or both. The Chesapeake and Ohio took us directly to Cincinnati, Washington and the Greenbrier in White Sulphur Springs, and not so directly to Chicago and New York. I had already been introduced to air travel with flights between Pittsburgh and Washington on a DC-3, and we now used commercial aircraft for trips to Pittsburgh. To and from the Columbus Airport, I had the use of the seven-seat company Cadillac and chauffeur. This convenience was one delightful fringe benefit of our corporate position, a practice Harold abandoned in all the three companies he subsequently headed.

We didn't anticipate any personal advantages from the medical residency we arranged for Klari (after having learned that she and Bill preferred to establish themselves in Chicago) at the Edgewater Beach Hospital. This step was necessary to enable her to take her Illinois Medical and Psychiatric State Board examinations. But while we lived in Portsmouth there was one occasion when it was to my advantage to have Klari as a resident there. I took one of the children to this hospital and to the doctor who made Klari's residency possible in the first place. Klari gave the young patient and me her utmost personal attention, before, during and after surgery. She completed her residency at a time when foreign graduates were not at all welcomed by the all-powerful American Medical Association establishment. Nevertheless, she passed her state boards the first time she took them, even though state medical authorities flunked many foreign doctors two or three times, often out of spite.

With respect to the children, Portsmouth was a prelude to the family's Golden Age. In fact, the growing-up years of all four children remained free of major problems. To me personally, these years were extremely challenging, rich in rewards. The children's physical and emotional development was always uppermost in my mind. But I also applied large doses of TLC (tender loving care) and common sense, bolstered by Gesell and Ilg's professional approach;[10] I felt equal to this task. Dr. Benjamin Spock, with whom we later played basketball on the Falk School parent team in Pittsburgh, published his ever-popular *Baby and Child Care* in 1946, too late for me to need it. One more important fact in connection with Portsmouth: it was time to plan another baby to complete our family. As it worked out, Ellen, our fourth and last child, was on the way when we moved back to Pittsburgh in 1949.

Family members visited us frequently, as they did wherever we lived. Parents, brothers and sisters-in-law, with their children and cousins from Chicago, all came at various times to see us in our small-town environment. For me, visits among in-laws and the younger generation of cousins were something to be promoted and enjoyed, even if from time to time there happened to be tensions between any two of us. All through my children's growing-up years, I created an atmosphere in my home that was conducive to family gatherings and taught by example expressions of affection for members of the family. To this day, I practice my belief that siblings and in-laws should be on the best of terms. In behalf of my children, unfortunately, I can no longer act. I must leave it to the next generation to do their utmost in carrying my ideals and examples forward into their own lives.

One example of our rising Jewish consciousness occurred in 1947, when Harold was already at his new post in Portsmouth but we as a family hadn't moved there yet. With the other leaders of the Jewish Community, we attended a regional conference called by the United Jewish Appeal in Huntington, West Virginia, forty miles from Portsmouth. Like hundreds of similar meetings across the country it was held to rally support for former concentration camp inmates trying to make their way to Palestine. Ours was a highly emotional and well-organized gathering; the drama of this moment in Jewish history and the speaker's fire and forensic talent combined to make the atmosphere a uniquely charged one. "There, but for the grace of God" had never been so applicable to my own case. Never before had I been so deeply touched by

Jewish history. To my everlasting regret, however, Israel's War of Liberation and the establishment of the State took place without my own personal involvement. Seven more years passed before I got myself into the act. Even so, the Huntington conference had an immediate sequel during our Portsmouth life.

Harold became chairman and active leader of the UJA fund-raising drive, and this meant that I was involved too. He was able to "negotiate" $10,000 in donations from scrap dealers to whom their relationship with Portsmouth Steel Company was essential. In addition, a phenomenal amount of $30,000 was collected within the Portsmouth Jewish Community, of which a sizable percentage was our own contribution.

Chapter 9

Return to Pittsburgh

Having been a big-city girl all my life, I welcomed the opportunity to return to Pittsburgh. A policy conflict with Cyrus Eaton, a perennial maverick in American industry and finance, provided the reason; the financial circumstances made it the right moment for departure. Portsmouth meant a great deal to us; it had been a most pleasant and, it so happened, a very advantageous interlude in our lives. Nevertheless, when our household possessions were loaded into the van and our two-car caravan left Portsmouth, I felt no sadness. Moving back up the Ohio to where the Allegheny and Monongahela converge meant going home to Pittsburgh. That is where I felt I belonged and where I would raise my family of four children. In our big Buick and even bigger company Cadillac, Harold's ex-Pittsburgher secretary, the boys, and we arrived one cold January afternoon. An inner glow of contentment accompanied us to the carriage entrance of the historic Schenley Hotel in Oakland, Pittsburgh's cultural center.

Eleanora Duse died there in 1924; guest performers, composers and conductors have stayed there when appearing in Pittsburgh. During my Pitt years, I set foot in the old-worldly elegance of the lobby and ballroom only on rare occasions; later, I dined only infrequently in the hotel's famous restaurant, where the cuisine was superb and Victor Saudek's orchestra played light classics and dance music. Always one looking from the outside in, I now felt the thrill of being a Schenley resident. We settled down in the comfort of a suite of two bedrooms, two baths and a sitting room, with Bernice Stanton[11] coming in to help with the children.

I was in my fifth month of pregnancy, and in a matter of a few weeks I was feeling uncomfortable. The two lively older boys and equally active two-year-old found the space, floors and elevators an invitation for mischief, in which they enthusiastically engaged themselves. On the whole, however, we were a very well-behaved family and endeared ourselves to everyone from the maitre d', Leo Stein (a fellow countryman of mine and a contemporary of my parents) through all the staff and service personnel. I enjoyed the elegance of my surroundings as well as the relative simplicity of our domestic arrangements; I was especially happy to be back with my parents and old friends.

The boys were immediately enrolled in the fourth and second grades of Falk School. Harold and I set out in search for the right house for our growing family. We inspected a number of fine homes of well-known Pittsburghers and finally chose the Robertson home at 5821 Aylesboro Avenue, an address that was to be ours for seventeen years. As the Ruttenberg home, it was the scene of countless joyous occasions, celebrations and a few tragic events as well, all of which left their indelible mark on me. This too was the home base of our children and the locale of the most intensive parenting of our lives.

It was a very special day when my daughter was born. I was told that the boys, upon hearing the news, dashed out into the street and shouted on neighbors' doorsteps, "It's a girl! It's a girl!" I felt truly fulfilled and saw my future happiness in my children assured.

Number 5821 Aylesboro Avenue stands on a lot with a 75-foot frontage and a depth of 150 feet. The house is slightly elevated from the street and has its main approach from a side driveway under a porte cochère. Supported by five sturdy Doric columns, it gives the house a distinctive appearance. Another outstanding feature of the property is the tall, thick hedge across its front and along one side. In the rear at the time was a two-car garage with chauffeur's quarters above it.

The grounds had been rather unimaginatively cared for, but under my mother's supervision Dominic transformed them into a lovely garden with colorful flower beds and clusters of flowering bushes and trees, successively blooming through three seasons in blazes of colors. The fig tree was buried each winter; a tamarisk in the front left corner, a rare specimen in Pittsburgh, proclaimed the grounds' continental connections.

Houses like this were nowhere else available and were not listed by agents. One of the main advantages was that the husband-and-wife team who had been in service with the Robertsons for many years were willing to stay on in the house and work for us. This was a singularly attractive proposition I would have been foolish to reject. Stella and Jesse were with us for five years, affording new and interesting life-styles for both of us. They had never before been as well paid and never before been treated with as much consideration as in our employ. The old coal furnace was the first appliance to be replaced, with a modern gas version; the kitchen of the twenties was next to be modernized. Stella was an accomplished cook; Jesse made an impressive houseman, butler and chauffeur. Between them, house and grounds were well cared for and many household and personal chores attended to. They loved being around the children, and Jesse took special pleasure in chauffeuring the three boys to and from school on the infrequent occasions when I allowed him this privilege. In 1950 our acquisition of a Cadillac made him strut with pride among his peers.

With all the household help, I still preferred to look after the children myself. Harold and I continued to be the involved parents we would have been in any case; in fact, being relieved of many mundane chores around the house and in the kitchen, we were actually more fully engaged in child rearing than would otherwise have been possible. For about fifteen years, I was an energetic and constant car pooler. After we finally prevailed upon Jesse to take a job in the steel mill—we thought the children were being spoiled—Stella stayed on for another year. This period of our lives came to an end about the time Ellen entered an all-day kindergarten. Among our friends, we were the only family in such an affluent household setup; Jesse and Stella were the only "couple" in the immediate neighborhood.

After Stella left, I experimented with all available types of household help: white living-in housekeepers including a Polish DP (displaced person), white and black day workers, and even an imported maid whose stock-in-trade was languages! Through Swedish friends in Monte Carlo, we learned about Helga, who wished to work in America. Having checked her references by mail, I once visited her in Paris during our negotiations. A wholesome Swedish beauty, she was from a good family, "in service" in Paris while perfecting her French. By the time she came to us some months later, she was just what I had in mind as a built-in French-speaking "companion" for the children. Helga, however, was more interested in perfecting her English than in doing housework or being a French tutor.

The children learned no French from her, but she learned a great deal of English from us all. Since Helga spent every hour, every day and every weekend when not on duty in search of pleasure, I was actually relieved when she decided to leave us. She had become more of a liability than an advantage. But as disappointed as I was in her performance and as concerned as I was for her social life, I couldn't help but admire this girl for her knack for languages and her single purpose!

In Portsmouth we had been a couple of big fish in a tiny pond; now we could retreat into relative anonymity as a couple of small fish in a super bowl. Harold's activities, including his writings, continued, however, to be newsworthy. A lengthy interview appeared in *U.S. News & World Report* in 1956. Articles about him and by him on the economy and labor-management relations were published in the *Nation, New Republic, Life, Harper's Magazine, Reader's Digest, Fortune, Harvard Business Review* and the local press. Harold's second book, *Self Developing America,* was published by Harper & Brothers in 1960. Our comings and goings and the children's honors became good copy in the Jewish press; sometimes even a book report or a communiqué appeared in print with my by-line.

In most of Harold's published works, there is also a tiny bit of me. I have always enjoyed reading everything he ever wrote for publication, and from the start I edited all that I read. At no time, however, did my contribution change the style or the meaning of his text, and Harold's writings remain uniquely his own.

We picked up the pieces of our social life in Pittsburgh with great ease. In fact, we were in a better position than before to pursue established friendships as well as make new ones. Our world of people had grown considerably since the Washington interlude; Portsmouth had also added a taste of big-business life-styles to it. We were now ready to enjoy relationships on several levels and in different contexts. Besides old college chums— whom we were to see less and less in the coming years—we still had friends dating from our union activities. Participating in the children's school affairs afforded us additional opportunities for a varied social life. Nor had we reason to neglect the personal contacts we already had among top management in industry. Among these, Colonel Rockwell's friendship became especially rewarding. Since the mid-fifties, through the Young Presidents' Organization, we also have had occasional pleasant connections with the Colonel's son, Al, and his wife, Connie.

Immediately upon moving into our house on Aylesboro Avenue, we joined Temple Sinai, a new Reform congregation in the city, and soon became active in its affairs. Our introduction into the life of Sinai was occasioned by Ellen's birth, which we celebrated six weeks later by formally naming her during the regular Shabat Eve service.

From the moment back in 1949 when we bought lots (more than we needed) in Sinai's Memorial Park to the present, we have made our presence felt in Temple in many concrete ways. Our activities in an artistic enhancement of our synagogue have continued through the years. After one baby naming, three funerals, three Bar Mitzvahs, four confirmations, two weddings in the family, a Torah dedication, an art auction and several significant art gifts, I feel a very real bond between us.

I have carried out many spot assignments and held several responsibilities in Sinai. For over five years, I was in charge of its growing library of Judaica and books of general interest. For many years I provided visual aid material and displays for various programs and projects, while for three years I edited the semimonthly *Bulletin,* a performance I am especially proud of. During many of the growing-up years of the children, I was active on the Religious School Board, serving as its secretary and chairman at one time or another. I was the first woman elected to the Board of Trustees (although I have never been a Sisterhood president) and served on the Board for a total of ten years. I was recently elected an honorary lifetime trustee.

The Aylesboro Avenue house was the right home for us at the right moment. There was an air of old-fashioned elegance about it, and it also provided a thoroughly practical arrangement for our needs. It was spacious, with five bedrooms upstairs. Two made ideal accommodations for our three growing boys, a third was Ellen's, one was the master suite, and the fifth served as a combination guest room and upstairs sitting room. One of the bathrooms was a ceramic *tour de force* of imported Italian tile in hues of lilac and apple green, with handsome gilded plumbing fixtures. It was a room to show off!

Within four years of our moving in, we relocated the dining room so that it would open into a new patio in the garden. We eliminated the butler's pantry, but we left the back stairway to the second and third floors as well as the downstairs powder room intact.

This major remodeling job on the main house was undertaken in conjunction with a total conversion of the chauffeur's quarters over the garage. My parents footed the bill for this, and in return they had a little dream house of their own. Quite by chance, we secured the services of a young, up-and-coming architect, Tasso Katselas, who had a reputation for being bold and imaginative. The only serious argument he gave us was his unwillingness to provide Mother with a small fixed window over the kitchen sink. But my mother was adamant, and she got her little lookout and with it a small ledge besides for her flowers and small plants. The apartment was complete in every respect: living room, dining area, eight-foot-long kitchen unit, bedroom, full bathroom and den. An outside stairway led to it, and, when trees were with foliage and in bloom, being there was like living in a treehouse. When we bought our present home, we were delighted to discover that Tasso had created 5100 Fifth Avenue at the time that our transactions on Aylesboro Avenue were in progress.

We had decided that I should be wholly responsible for the house and garage apartment remodeling. Tasso was willing, and I was also lucky to have a master carpenter who was patient and a born teacher of his craft. As contractor, I dealt with all craftsmen, the most difficult of them being the plumber. I bought all materials from building supply firms and from hardware and plumbing fixture wholesalers, and I saw to it that men and materials appeared as needed and as scheduled. To conserve time and personnel—and thus reduce expenses—it was essential that I bring maximum efficiency to my task. There were only a very few instances of faulty scheduling, and I recall no significant mistakes. Garden clubbing wasn't "my thing"; being chief contractor on my own house-building project was. It was an exciting involvement, and I loved every moment of it. There is literally something more than seventeen years of my life in the property at 5821 Aylesboro Avenue.

Chapter 10

Golden Age of Family

During the years when the children were young and getting in and out of stages and phases, through their mid-teens, my time for ongoing extracurricular activity was limited. I limited it myself, for that was my understanding of my role as mother. I wanted to give the best of me to the children's physical, emotional, and character development; I wanted to be available to them at all times when needed. For me, these were the joys and responsibilities of motherhood.

While the children were in Falk School, through the eighth grade, they entertained their friends a great deal and hosted many parties at home. Among the liveliest, I recall especially folk-dancing evenings and birthday parties. Three social functions relating to Bar Mitzvahs were held at home, too, continuing the festivities in Temple that included the religious service in the morning followed by a simple catered luncheon.

The children all had equal intellectual capacity, being in the lower levels of the superior range. They were serious students and had their own ideas of how to spend their extracurricular time. I was as supportive as I knew how to be; I took pride in all their achievements and honors. They all had their moments of rebellion against parents, authority and home standards, some more, some less. But only one child slipped into a contrary stage that was more intense and lasted longer than I considered reasonable. I held a short-term point of view on this matter, which proved to be of no help at all.

His teenage nonperformance in and out of school and at home, coupled with constant moodiness, distressed me no end. My misery was also cause for further difficulties between him and us and between Harold and myself. Klari and my friend Vera Tisza, both psychiatrists, were my confidantes during this time, and I cannot thank them enough for their sensitive and sympathetic dealings with me. They listened patiently and tried to guide me. However, I was able to follow their advice only rarely. The problem in the family was compounded by Harold's assessing the situation from angles totally different from mine. And so, while on the whole those years were the Golden Age of Family, my acute concern for the one son during his teens added a troubled aspect to this otherwise happy period of my life.

The high points of my deep emotions for Eddie were his wedding, his rabbinical ordination at Hebrew Union College–Jewish Institute of Religion in 1972, and his achievement of a Ph.D. degree five years later. The ordination weekend, June 2–4, was "ours" as well as "his." As proud parents, we extended hospitality on this auspicious occasion in Cincinnati to our children, their spouses, Father, our in-laws, and a few dear friends. Today, Eddie is a first-rate scholar and finds contentment in his profession. Most recently we were honored by him in his address at his installation in his new post as rabbi.

Charlie's and Jimmie's graduations from Massachusetts Institute of Technology in 1961 and 1963, and their extensive musical activities, among others, gave me much pleasure. I was particularly moved at Charlie's picturesque lakeside wedding in 1965 and when he earned his law degree (J.D.) from American University, at age thirty-seven and already a Ph.D. (New York University). Besides his wedding, Jimmie's *shofar*[12]-blowing years of his youth and his professional appearance once with the Pittsburgh Symphony as a trumpet player are what gave me emotional lifts. Hired for two performances upon audition by Maestro William Steinberg himself, Jim at seventeen per-

1. My parents' wedding photo–1913

2. Gymnazium student–1925

3. New York Public Library Lion and I–arrival in the USA–1927

4. In labor–Philip Murrary, Harold and I–1940

5. In the little pond: Harold, the industrialist and I–Portsmouth, Ohio–1947

6. Golden Age of Family—1950

7. Golden age of family— 1953

8. With Carlos Boyer in Madrid–1969

9. With Ellen in Florence–1965

10. Unsinkable me–in the Dead Sea, Israel–1968

11. About to board the Jet Commander to fly it to Israel—Nice—1967

12. Klari on my Jerusalem balcony–1977

13. With Agam in Paris–1969

14. With Castel in Jerusalem–1972

15. With Fima at 5100 Fifth Avenue, Pittsburgh–1973

16. With Gross and Bezem–Penthouse, Pittsburgh–1970

17. Double exposure–portrait with the view from the balcony in Jerusalem–1972 (before the touch-up)

18. and 19. To and from Jericho–my soldier shuttle during the
Yom Kippur War–1973

20. With Ze'ev Sharef and Harold at inauguration of Liberty Bell Garden in Jerusalem (informal and unofficial)–1978

21. After-concert party in our Jerusalem home: Lorin Maazel, Ellen Hirsch and I–1977

formed under his baton in 1958 in Mahler's Symphony no. 2 in C-minor *(Resurrection)*.

As to Ellie, here was a child who was the least contrary, most cooperative, most thoughtful of others. She, too, was an excellent student and a conscientious youngster. I especially appreciated her wholesome outpouring of affection towards me in her childhood and youth. A Brandeis University graduate, she earned her M.S.W. (master of social work) degree from Columbia University. Her wedding in 1971 was a highlight of my life.

I myself was always demonstrative by nature, a kiss-and-hug bug. I still am. Neither was I a placid mother, leaving the acquisition of good manners and good habits and character development to chance. I viewed my role as mother not only in loving and giving terms but also as that of an active guide and expediter; I believed in the "love and limits" theory. That my definite ideas would occasionally come into conflict with the children's was something I took for granted. There were instances when they and I were on a collision path that I regret to this day. On the other hand, very often my notions of what was appropriate or desirable were not too actively contested. Such as: a parent should be visible at boy-girl parties in the preteen and teen years. Or surveillance of television viewing or double-feature movies or pool-playing after school, or proper dressing for the occasion. I told the children then, and in retrospect I still maintain, that I wasn't competing in a popularity contest. I was merely trying to be the best mother I knew how to be. I can honestly say that their accomplishments and character development over the years have proved me right. That the children apparently lack constancy in their feelings for us and for each other in their adult years I can only see as a non sequitur. I am baffled and distressed by this turn of events, but I do not feel responsible for it.

In one area of rearing the all-American child, I was woefully deficient. This was baseball, to which I must confess an unconquerable aversion. I learned to like American college football when I was a freshman at Pitt, being obliged to attend all home games in order to pass a "school spirit" test. But baseball remains foreign to me, and, on the rare occasions that I am exposed to it, I find it dull and boring. On one historic occasion in 1960, I was included in a party of baseball-fan friends attending the seventh game of the World Series. Bill Mazeroski hit a home run in the final inning and won the world championship for the Pittsburgh Pirates. The crowd went wild; pandemonium broke loose. And I just stared and wondered what on earth was happening. . . .

Children in our home were always visible and audible but were brought up to respect adults' need for privacy as well. Practice on the piano, double bass, clarinet, trumpet or recorder was, however, a welcome sound at almost any time. Radio listening was somewhat rationed but persisted for several years after television sets were standard equipment among the neighbors. I saw no reason to rush into the TV world of distraction and considered aural addiction to the Lone Ranger on his Hi Ho Silver, and Jack Armstrong, the All-American Boy, far more wholesome than being mesmerized by sounds and sights of mediocre TV broadcasting. When television made its delayed appearance in our home, there were rules about program selection and amount of time allotted to viewing. The rules might have been strict, but there were occasional lapses too. In those days, also, for sheer entertainment, there was much that parents and children could watch and enjoy together. And we did. We all loved Lucy and Jack Benny.

The sound of children playing inside and outside was frequently augmented by neighboring children. There was much horseplay around the grounds, basketball by the garage, football passing, and pitch-'n'-catch everywhere. From time to time we also had badminton and croquet games going on, in which I too could participate. Harold was the expert in football and baseball and showed endless patience in both. He also taught the children how to ride a bicycle and to skate.

There were trips to and from camps and visits thereto, which were always combined with family excursions. There were side trips to nearby caverns, the Virginia countryside, and Sky Line Drive. En route to and from Saranac Lake, New York, we explored oil country around Titusville, Pennsylvania, the Thousand Islands, Hyde Park, and other sites of interest. One summer our target was Washington, D.C., where we visited all the major sites together with the Osler (Grace and Dave) family, whose three daughters were compatible in age with our sons. Once we shared a family excursion to the Canadian Laurentians for a holiday, and another time we all enjoyed Montreal's tourist offerings for a long weekend. Niagara Falls, American and Canadian, complete with *Maid of the Mist* and the nearby fort, was not neglected either among family vacations.

When the oldest son was already an MIT man and the other children were sixteen, eleven and nine, I accompanied them to Williamsburg and Monticello. They loved it, even if I did rush us to the grounds immediately upon arrival instead of lounging around in the motel room listening to a baseball game. I may not have won a popularity contest that evening either, but, as the sun was setting and oil lamps were being turned on, we had a good look at the activities in this eighteenth-century town restored at great expense and with meticulous care. We spent still another several hours there the next day, besides making time for a refreshing swim and the inevitable pitch-'n'-catch, before driving on to Monticello.

Charlie once shared an extensive business trip to the West Coast, the Southwest and Mexico with his father. Jim spent one year at Stanford University in Palo Alto earning his M.Sc., and Eddie had one semester in San Francisco as a Macy stock boy during his Antioch College days. Haight-Ashbury was provocatively near by the younger boy, but it held no appeal for him. Ellie's big trip in the States by herself was to Phoenix, where she went to visit her former neighbor.

By the time we could afford foreign travel for the children, the older boys were in their early twenties, and so their first trip abroad was made in each other's company. They had been buddies all their lives, and this jaunt in Europe and Israel was on the whole a very successful one for them. They later returned to Israel to participate in our family summer at the seashore in Herzlia. Another summer Charlie devoted to Crossroads Africa ("building bridges" in Nigeria). The other three focused on Israel according to their own preferences: Eddie in kibbutz Ein Dor, Ellie studying for a semester in the Leo A. Baeck High School in Haifa, and Jimmie working in the Bureau of Vital Statistics in Jerusalem as a young professional statistician.

On other trips abroad, Ellie accompanied us on the Route Napoleon from Nice through Grenoble to Lake Annecy; in Scotland and Monaco; to Lyons, Athens, Rome, Rotterdam, Venice. She also sailed with us on the Greek ship *Enotria* from Piraeus to Haifa once, this two-and-a-half-day boat ride being especially noteworthy for the presence of New York and Belgian Hassidim, who accompanied their revered leader, the Szatmar Rebbe, en masse. Still another time, she spent a summer with me in Jerusalem; during this period she was enrolled briefly in an Israeli camp with cousin Dorith and had the mumps in solitary confinement in the King David Hotel. In 1967, immediately after the Six Day War, Jimmie and Ellie joined their father in a personal victory celebration with family and friends in Israel. Ellen's Vienna-Budapest tour I reserve for later mention in connection with my own story.

Now that my oldest granddaughter is twelve, I begin to think about traveling with grandchildren "when the time and their ages are right." In 1961, when Eddie was fourteen and Ellie twelve and the circumstances were right, we embarked on a varied summer program of travel, camping, sightseeing and studies for all the children. The plans evolved from their own interests and suggestions and were carried out with much collective enthusiasm and all the organizing and coordinating skills I could bring to this ambitious project. The older boys toured Europe and spent a couple of weeks in Israel. At about the same time I sailed with the younger children on the *New Amsterdam;* visited with our Swedish friends, the Lundbergs, in Monaco; and met the boys coming back from Israel in Montreux. Here I left the young ones for a month in a French-speaking camp, during which time Charlie, Jimmie, my eighty-one-year-old father, and I attended the University of Lausanne summer school to study French. We all toured the countryside, visited the castle of Chillon, sailed on

Lake Leman, and explored Geneva thoroughly. Harold joined us on the last two weeks of this super–family holiday.

After camp and French studies, the older boys continued their European tour; the two younger children and I went our own way, by train to Luxembourg, on to Amsterdam and then to London. Here, Eddie was the expert in getting us around everywhere by bus and underground, and he excelled in all financial transactions, which in their premetric state were rather bothersome for me. We had a most moving experience in Amsterdam: I shall never forget my twelve-year-old Ellen coming through the fake bookcase in the apartment where Anne Frank had been hiding, looking very much like Anne herself. The sight of her, very close to Anne in age, brought home the tragedy of the whole Jewish experience of the Hitler times. As a result, I began a collection of Anne Frank books in different languages. Within a year or two, friends, relatives and business associates around the world had sent me copies from their countries that I couldn't buy myself in the States. I have more than a literary interest in this eighteen-book collection of Anne Frank, even though only three are in languages I am competent to read.[13]

Other great pleasures, in addition to trips abroad, were two holidays in Florida. In the winter of 1951–52, the children had an unending series of colds. I therefore took them to Miami Beach for three weeks at spring recess. Together with my parents, we settled in one of the less glamorous hotels, at Forty-first Street on Collins Avenue, in a suite with two bedrooms and a sitting room, and dedicated ourselves to sea and sun, for pleasure and benefit of all of us. A similar visit took place in 1955, when Harold and I were returning from our South American tour of "duty." We met the children from the frigid north, the younger ones already having spent a week under the care of their grandparents, and enjoyed another successful late-winter holiday en famille.

During the flight from Buenos Aires to Lima, in a DC-6 (before jets!) through the jagged edges of the Andes, I decided the time was right to discuss the children's forthcoming summer camp prospects. A new direction was indicated, I maintained. Enough of camps with primarily swimming and baseball emphases, enough of leather links and loops in crafts, enough of traditional counselor-in-training programs. At sixteen and four-teen, as interested as they were in music, Charlie and Jimmie were ready to broaden their horizons and be in the company of more mature young people. Richard Karp, founder and longtime director of the Pittsburgh Opera, and his wife, Ilse, with a staff of musicians and other performing arts experts, offered the camping experience I sought for the children. It turned out to be a smashing success for them for two years. Even the younger two were willing to participate in this extraordinary program the second season.

I considered the children's summers at Deerwood Music Camp an enriching experience for them. The Deerwood Symphony Orchestra played for the Saranac Lake clientele, with Jim on trumpet and Charlie on double bass. I also promoted a couple of summer sessions for the three younger children at Chatham College Music Day Camp, which was in the heart of residential Pittsburgh and only a few blocks from our home. Here Jim could play and coach much tennis and toot much trumpet, while Eddie and Ellie did what they liked on the program.

Tennis, ice-skating, and swimming were the sports I encour-aged most, even though the first two were then out of step with the popular trend. Only twenty years later did the children realize that tennis, the nemesis of their teens, had become the overwhelming favorite active sport of the nation, with ice-skating also making great strides in popularity. Today, Eddie is a tennis buff and enjoys opera. Jimmie, the most musical, plays first trumpet in the Westchester Symphony Orchestra. Ellie switched to flute and has an enviable collection of classical music records. The older boys give their daughters music lessons; Charlie is taking clarinet lessons again. They may not be much better than wobbly on skates, but all can play tennis well; also a good game of chess, their grandfather's legacy.

I believed in using our home, all of it, not sparing it. Overseas business friends were entertained in reciprocity to their generous acts of hospitality to us abroad, or in fact predating them; friends and relatives passing through Pittsburgh stayed with us. Celebrations of all happy occasions were held in the home.

Holiday meals were frequently attended by in-laws or foreign visitors. Seder nights were especially times for including a close friend or two who might not be invited elsewhere. Children's post-confirmation fetes and Ellie's sixteenth birthday party were teen-age affairs I recall well. Three family-oriented celebrations I shall never forget: my parents' fortieth and forty-fifth wedding anniversaries, which we observed in the midst of family and friends, theirs and ours; and the last big occasion on Aylesboro, our own fiftieth-birthday party, which we gave ourselves. In addition to fifty or more American guests and the children, two Israeli cousins were in attendance, giving the party an even more festive air. Dafna had just arrived for a two-year stay as a kindergarten specialist at the Hebrew Institute, and Guszti was also our guest for a six-week visit at this time. They were the first two of a series of foreign relations whose trips to this country I promoted or financed.

The fiftieth-birthday party was in August, three months after the actual date. We wanted to celebrate when children would be at home after summer job, camp or travel; guests from abroad still with us; and the garden at its colorful best. We discouraged gifts. We did, however, receive many kind expressions of regard from friends in the form of contributions to our favorite charities. A shopping cart finished in anodized gold with a plaque attached to the handle showing our names and the dates of our birth is still a rolling reminder of this happy event.

The shopping cart, as well as a table model of it, are also reminders of the five years Harold and I spent involved in the affairs of the United Steel and Wire Company. Promotion of the company's welfare took us abroad many times between 1964 and 1969. As President, Chairman of the Board and Chief Executive Officer, Harold demonstrated again his well-known capacity to manage a sizable industrial enterprise.

Our intrafamily relationships were spontaneous and loving, demonstrating intimacies as well as disagreements. Gentle care shown by the older ones toward the younger was the norm. But physical combat wasn't ruled out among them either. The children could always express anger and disappointment, and what I tried to do in such cases was to patch up physical and emotional bruises as sympathetically as I could. Bringing up children wasn't even then a simple, routine matter, but I believed that we couldn't possibly be less than the happiest parents in our older years. As a first step in that direction, I couldn't wait for them to find their mates and be married.

There were many beautiful occasions during the Golden Age of Family that were related to happy togetherness for the children, and between them and us and very often also their grandparents. We played games and worked puzzles. We read to them a great deal from infancy on. We attended circuses, amusement shows, and plays together. We played badminton, croquet and ball and swam together. I was an eager Cub Scout den mother and participated enthusiastically in grade school affairs. Harold went on Scout outings and was active with the children in all indoor and outdoor games.

A family visit in New York in 1952 on the occasion of my uncle's and aunt's golden wedding anniversary was a memorable one. My parents, Harold and I and the two older boys attended this milestone event, staying in the elegant Pierre Hotel where the gala celebration took place. As "poor" relations from the hinterland, we felt quite comfortable mingling with true affluence. Father relished being my cousins' only and favorite uncle present, and I got devilish pleasure from being accepted as a success story.

Twenty-three years later, Harold and I attended Kaplans' fiftieth anniversary party, which was scheduled on a date most convenient to the largest number of their far-flung family. I was alerted months in advance so that I could tailor my travels accordingly. The earlier Manheim affair had an indelible impact on me. From then on, anniversaries and family gatherings have had an even greater meaning for me than before. I now wondered how my own fortieth wedding anniversary will pass into history. An inner compulsion tells me to share important milestones in life with others, those I care about. This is one way—not the only way—happiness in family is spelled out for me. I feel equally desolate, on the other hand, when deprived of a celebration that would normally be indicated. Through the years, I have had my portion both of joy shared and of pain inflicted by joy denied.

The Golden Age of Family was marred most poignantly by the death of my mother at not quite seventy-two. The cancer she discovered in Cordova (during my father's Spanish assignment for Westinghouse) and that was operated on in Rome took its tragic toll. When Harold and I learned of Mother's illness, we were at the Brussels Worlds Fair en route to Israel. We all decided to meet promptly in Rome, where we had proper referrals and where Mother felt comfortable with respect to the practice of medicine. Father terminated his affairs in Cordova, and Harold and I stayed on for two weeks after Mother's hospitalization and "enjoyed," to the extent we could, the beautiful spring air on Via Veneto. During this period, cousin Louise (the youngest Manheim) spent several days with us trying to overcome her divorce blues. She was welcome company to Mother and us, and we were just what she sought for diversion. The Excelsior Hotel was never as convenient, the sidewalk cafés were never as pleasant, and the Trevi fountain was never as impressive as then, when needed for our collective morale. We accompanied my parents home.

When the case became "terminal" and Mother was in and out of the hospital, she was cared for in her own home, which had been converted into a veritable clinic. She died there after massive cobalt radiation therapy, within a year of surgery. I was at her bedside, holding her hand.

I had already seen death at close range: I was the one who found my mother-in-law, seven years earlier, slumped in her favorite chair, victim of a massive coronary. But my mother's death had a devastating impact on me. Only the fact that I had my own growing family and now Father to look after kept me from utter despair. Death after all is part of life, I learned.

My Golden Age of Family didn't remain static. Does it ever? Anywhere? Children grow up, young parents become middle aged and beset with concerns of their own. Couples grow old together or they grow apart. We all pass through many phases as we mature and age, acquiring psychological or emotional bruises along the way. Unfortunately, these tend to overshadow the joys and satisfactions that are coincidental with them. Also, young people, in the name of sibling rivalry and search for self-identity, have their own difficulties in their growing-up years. Many resolve their problems, developing closer-than-ever family relationships in their adulthood. Some, on the other hand, have a diminishing need for family (How they delude themselves!) and drift away from one another. A few even end up alienated.

Before I continue with my story, which contains additional joyous events and bright highlights, I shall speak briefly on another aspect of my family life.

May, 1974, was a significant month of milestones for me. Had it not been for Father's sudden physical collapse, a birthday celebration would have been a happy prospect. As it was, Harold's and my sixtieth, falling on the eighth day after Father's funeral, turned out to be one of the most wrenching moments of my life, for it brought all the current unpleasantness within the family into focus. Already acutely conscious of the strains among us, now I could no more use euphemisms to describe them.

I could no longer explain the deteriorating situation by calling it "generational" and dismiss it. As "just another phase" I considered it too long and too distressing. Not all the incidents have been equally painful, not all the hurts of equal measure. In any case, within fifteen months after the special birthday event, their total impact on me—at this particular time of my life—was absolutely devastating. I was vulnerable. Facing this crushing phase of my life was just too much for me. And so, when my rose-colored optimism no longer served me well, I coped less and less.

In addition to brooding over the state of the family, I also had at this time the responsibility for the execution of my father's will. A manifold task, a "first" for me, in itself a depressing one. So, for relief of stresses and a more effective way of dealing with my deep depression, I went to a psychiatrist related to me only professionally. The sessions continued for over a year and a half, interrupted only for trips to the children, to holiday spots or to Jerusalem. In speculating on the success of the therapy, I wonder if the amount of Librium and Kleenex consumed were an accurate indication. . . . In any case, I readily acknowledge that both the therapist and the therapy were very helpful.

I pay attention to all the positive messages from all the

children. That there are signs at all I find reassuring. In fact, in recent months there have been two major indications that we may yet recapture the old gold of the Golden Age of our Family. Therefore, I contemplate ideal relationships in the children's adult and our remaining years, appending a sensible, realistic definition of "ideal" to my expectations. As this book goes to press, they are very likely to be in the making. I keep all doors open!

One professional perspective on my parent-child dilemma might be that Harold and I were a "tough act to follow". Perhaps currently, we are less and less so. During the ten years while intra-family relations in general were eroding, I learned to appreciate the occasional good moments and small kindnesses, whenever and from whomever they emanated. As philosophical as I am about hurt, I am not on the other hand false enough to deny it. Unfortunately, in our culture, there seems to be a double standard in vogue now: a parent can be told off or totally ignored, but he/she jeopardizes the children's good will if he/she expresses his/her distress or disappointment. A parent overlooks and readily forgives; the children are less so inclined. I can read all the articles and books on the subject, I can hear therapists' diagnoses and I can poll friends about their own experiences. Just the same, I am sensitive and I endured. To which young people these days respond, "That's your problem", conveniently disposing of the matter.

When we have everything going for us as a family, why are some contacts either rare or hardly beyond shallow formalities? (Harold's and my sixty-fifth birthday celebration is not yet in perspective but I am already happily judging it as *the* turn-around in the life of our family.) When we are in a fortunate position to overcome distances easily and without financial strain, why are we not closer to one another? Why do they so seldom and so little care about each other's comings and going, each other's milestone events? Why is one's freedom of choice more important than parents' or siblings' sensitivities? Why, for so long, no two-, three-, four-way family get-togethers? If a closeknit family exists anywhere, why not in ours? And why not sooner than later?

On the one hand, I have a great deal to be grateful for. Our health and each other we have, Harold and I. Financially secure, we live well and enjoy a great many material and cultural benefits. We lovingly raised four children[14] to be good human beings and attractive personalities. We can justly be proud of their accomplishments and talents, which are legion. They have all attained the level in their professional and private lives that they desired. They all married within the faith. They have given us nine wonderful grandchildren, their greatest gift to us, our guarantee for immortality.

And now, on the other hand, where is the tender human element, the sense of Family, the touch of understanding and affection that binds kin together in their adult years? There does not seem to be enough of this precious stuff. That is, not enough of it showing and at work. This is what I miss among the children. This is what I wish to live long enough to see, feel and enjoy.

Chapter 11

Extra Curriculum

I drifted into Hadassah through friends. Sympathy with its purpose and objectives made my involvement deeper as time rolled on. I made my contribution on many different levels to the extent that I was able: at first small assignments, then vice-presidencies in different departments, finally the presidency of my group of about five hundred members, from 1962 to 1964. Even after this I continued to work on isolated projects, but my growing interest in other activities precluded any sustained involvement. Nor did I see myself as a leader of any consequence in a women's organization, however worthy its goals. My financial support to Hadassah nonetheless has never wavered. As a further gesture of solid attachment to Hadassah's role on the Israeli scene in medical services, research and social welfare, I became a life member and, hoping to pass my interest on to her, made my daughter one as well.

Hadassah was a great teacher to me, helping to develop further some of the organizational talents that for almost fifteen years had been concentrated on domestic duties and child rearing. In my view, communal activity along structured lines, such as Jewish philanthropy, is an exacting art. Being successful in both interpersonal relationships and desired results reflects achievement in both approaches. I took my volunteer duties (as limited as they were) seriously, applying myself to each task with a combination of tried tradition and a bit of unorthodoxy. Delegating responsibilities, conducting meetings, writing reports, and speaking extemporaneously formed a demanding challenge; I was grateful for the learning process thus provided. The Hadassah experience, together with the earlier debate activities at Pitt, has given me the confidence for the occasional public speaking that I have done in recent years. There is nothing like learning while doing.

It was as President of the Stardrill Keystone Company (a pioneer company, manufacturing water well drilling machines dating back to the nineteenth century) that Harold became eligible for the Young Presidents Organization. We enjoyed our association with the YPO[15] right through our forties and Harold's two companies until his mandatory retirement from an active role at age forty-nine. Now that we are YPO Forty-Niners, the former two or three social events a year have been reduced to one Christmastime affair. I have fond memories of a YPO convention just outside Phoenix at which Jack Benny and Mary Livingston were with us as entertainers for a whole weekend and where we luxuriated in the ultimate in resort ambience, including freshly flown-in leis of orchids from Hawaii for everyone.

One other ultimate in elbow rubbing with celebraties was the 1950 reunion of the Steel Division of the War Production Board, held at the Greenbrier. The Duke and Duchess of Windsor were paying one of their periodic visits to the States, and this time they were guests of Robert R. Young of the Chesapeake and Ohio Railroad. We (the YPO) invited the royal couple to be our guests at the formal banquet and ball. I have visited Schoenbrunn, Versailles, and other assorted royal palaces before and after this event; I have watched ex-kings and queens play cards in Estoril. But spending an evening dining and dancing "with" ex–King Edward (uncrowned as he was) and his Wallis, and Harold teeing off just behind him the next morning, were all clearly an extraordinary occasion.

When the 1956 Hungarian refugees began to appear in Pittsburgh, my knowledge of their language became extremely useful. I threw myself into work with the Jewish Children's and Family Society, helping the refugees acclimate themselves. I worked as long and as often as I was needed. I was indispensable as an interpreter between social worker and client when the client knew no Yiddish or English—which was nearly always the case. In fact, the clients soon learned to take advantage of my services and engaged me more often and in more personal ways than the professionals of the agency ever imagined. Over a period of about two years, I dedicated much time and effort to the integration of nine new American families in Pittsburgh. One couple, whose lives are a true success story, remain to this day friends of ours.

There were many aggravating as well as humorous aspects to my involvement with the refugees. On the one hand, I was taken to task by the executive director for my critical evaluation of some of the agency's methods. On the other hand, in assisting two clients with the formalities of marriage, I earned the wrath of the happy couple. Giveaway shows on TV then enjoyed great popularity, and "Bride for a Day" was a favorite among the refugees. On this program a lucky couple was chosen to be married on TV, and a flood of valuable gifts accrued to them for their cooperation.

When my couple saw cameras in the judge's chambers—which I had arranged so that their human interest story could have television and newspaper coverage—they arrived at the inescapable conclusion that they were on a televised giveaway program. Where were the refrigerator, television set, grand piano and Caribbean cruise? Obviously, according to them, they had been cheated: the judge and I had shared the loot.

One 1956 Hungarian refugee whom I befriended I found, not through the Pittsburgh Jewish Federation, but motor-scooting in Rome, where he was employed in air-conditioning the Pope's summer villa. A nephew of friends of my parents, he was anxious to come to the United States to further his career. However, he no longer had refugee status; so it was a question of making his immigration possible through normal channels. Because he was a skilled draftsman, Harold's offer of a job at Stardrill Keystone Drilling Company seemed to be the solution to his problem. Just the same, it took much correspondence, a great deal of stateside red tape, and my personal intervention with the Hebrew Immigrant Aid Society (HIAS) in Rome before Steve could come to America.

At the end of the 1950s, the plight of the Rumanian Jews became a matter of concern. Most of my Hungarian relatives who had lived in Rumania were by now settled in Jerusalem, but one family remained behind: my father's younger sister, her widowed daughter-in-law, and her grandson, Tibi (now Gabi for Gabriel), then still in medical school. They had been trying for years to leave Rumania, but emigration to Israel was strictly limited. (Not until the early sixties did the gates become more flexible.) Tibi's appeal for assistance touched my heart and moved me to action. He proposed a scheme whereby a Frenchman in Nice would make their move to Israel possible via France. I promptly engaged in correspondence with the Frenchman, supplying the necessary notarized declarations and assurances. At the same time, without one single intermediary, I made immediate contact with the Rumanian Embassy in Washington. I succeeded in being received by a high-ranking attaché who made me believe he was the Ambassador's eyes, ears and right hand. He also assured me that Tibi's case was going to be handled in a special way, on grounds of family reunification. He was so going to instruct his government.

Whether it was the Frenchman or the Rumanian attaché who would have resolved Tibi's emigration, I shall never know. Anyway, this became an academic question when Tibi and my aunt telephoned us from Vienna. We told them what they already knew about their "rights," about HIAS and about the Jewish Agency. Within a couple of days, the three of them were on their way to start a new life in Israel.

One new American family in whose integration I played a small but welcome part was George Rocher and his wife, children and mother-in-law. He was neither a refugee nor in need when he appeared in Pittsburgh. If a man's profession had anything to do with steel (or steel fabricating) and he was a Hungarian (even though he had lived in Paris for many years), there was just one thing to do with him: put him in touch with Kitty and Harold. The telephone rang (the call was from our rabbi's office), and George was at once on his way to our house—in time for a second breakfast. His briefcase full of credentials, and his self-confident manner as well as his utter sincerity, made him absolutely credible. George, a metallurgist, brought with him a chemical process valuable to American industry. In no time at all, Harold was able to open every business door he needed; I did what I can do best: help to integrate the family into the life of Pittsburgh. George also brought with him means that enabled the family to start life with advantages very few newcomers have. Ours was just a chance encounter. But our Temple became their Temple; some of our friends became their friends. Once Bergen-Belsen sweethearts, today Agnes and George live in relative affluence and lead a beautiful life. We were, for them, in the right place at the right time.

We were also useful to at least half a dozen other persons whose cases were brought to my attention, in providing them with affidavits of support. Not once were we ever put to the acid test.

Family, outside activities, entertaining and travel overlapped so much that it never occurred to me to look for a job; there was no economic necessity for one, nor did I seem to need it for my own self-expression. There was, however, one notable exception to my no-job career at this time of my life. In February, 1962, the Pittsburgh Board of Education engaged a team of ten housewives to grade English themes at Allderdice High School. There were many applicants; the selection process included stiff examinations and a personal interview. Of the ten chosen, nine were younger than I and still had young children at home; they were all trying to break out of the confines of their homes. We were all college graduates and, according to newspaper accounts, had "strong English backgrounds."

My theme-reading career was a curious topic of conversation among my friends. To my utter relief, my family was impressed by my "devotion to duty." I also had a built-in convenience both years, as my son Eddie gladly picked up my weekly batch of themes and returned them, read and graded; again and again.

This pickup and delivery system suffered a temporary halt when Harold and I took off one February for Miami Beach for a two-week holiday. There I continued to analyze, correct, comment on and grade senior students' English themes, somewhere around eighty or ninety of them. Between social engagements, on the beach and by the side of the pool, I was busy teaching teenagers how to write better English compositions.

I enjoyed tremendously not being a volunteer for a change, even if I was earning only $2.00 an hour at a time when the minimum wage in the country was $1.15 for unskilled labor. Of the grand salary of about $30.00 I grossed during the Florida holiday, I spent at least $3.00 on airmail and special delivery stamps! This job experience of mine also involved the additional entry of $480.00 as income on our joint tax return in two successive years. Neither Harold nor our accountant was especially pleased about this.

I didn't see myself as working on my highest intellectual level correcting English themes of high schoolers. Having had a taste of librarianship in its simplest form in Temple Sinai's Falk Library, I decided to earn my master's degree in library science. Both the qualifying degree and the education in its pursuit would be worthy goals.

I never viewed myself as "just a housewife." From 1940 on, I listed myself as a "homemaker" in the federal census. More visibly yet, I am a homemaker according to my passport. A subtle difference? Perhaps. To me, it is a way of making a point. I had visions of being an older woman on the Pitt campus competing with fresh young minds and eventually being employed, part time of course, in an educational institution, hospital, or industrial enterprise. At Pitt, a new Office of Continuing Education for Women was luring women into expanding professions to give them self-confidence and job opportunities. In February, 1964, therefore, I applied for admission to the Library School. I also made some simple calculations as to timing. Since the catalogue didn't indicate that the course of studies must be finished within a specified time, I was prepared to attend semesters as and when I wasn't called overseas, for as long as it would take.

I felt the excitement of waiting as keenly as I remembered my
three sons feeling when they applied to the colleges of their
choice. I too succeeded, as in March the dean informed me that
he was "pleased to report that [my] application for entrance to
Graduate Library School has been approved by the committee on
Admissions." All summer I was the proudest fifty-year-old
woman around and looked forward eagerly to my studies in the
fall. However, something unexpected happened to interfere with
my future professional life. More accurately, it eliminated it.

Harold had just acquired the United Steel and Wire Company
and became its President, Chief Executive Officer, and majority
stockholder. The company, one of whose chief products was
shopping carts, was invited to exhibit in an international trade fair
in Vienna. Should I go with Harold and shopping carts, visit
Vienna and most likely also return to my native city? Or should I
stick to my studies and take that first important step toward an
advanced degree? Beethoven, Mozart and Johann Strauss
beckoned, as did the Danube, Schoenbrunn and *Sacher Torte*. My
mind was swimming with exciting prospects. It was a tough
decision and, while I deeply regretted giving up my M.A., I was
more than compensated for my loss.

In Vienna, I was official hostess of our company's exhibit; I
met diplomats and, for the first time, sales engineers from behind
the Iron Curtain. I dressed up our shopping carts with real
merchandise—staples, canned goods, soft drinks, wine, and even
a life-size doll in the baby seat. We were a sensation, and the
United States' image of affluence and gadgetry was safe in our
hands and in our carts. We did some sight-seeing and undertook
two major personal journeys when not actually minding the store.

One was an excursion to Bratislava and another a weekend in
Budapest. Each had emotional undertones, but each was unique
in its own way. By telephone I was able to reach Elvira, a cousin
whom I had never met. On Yom Kippur, which fell within this
period, we refrained from work. Instead, we drove (though this
too is contrary to tradition) to nearby Bratislava, just over the
border in Czechoslovakia, to meet Elvira and her family.

We had no breakfast that morning (a fast day), but, so as not to
appear empty handed, we took with us a large basket of

delicatessen items and Israeli wines. Neither did Elvira receive us empty handed. However, we skipped the welcome meal for the moment and spent hours just filling each other in with our personal histories. In the drama of the occasion, we felt no remorse in breaking the fast together hours ahead of time. We then took a short ride about the city and walked to the synagogue, stopping briefly for a reminder of this Holy Day. We also strolled along the Danube and took a light supper in Elvira's favorite café. We were crushed, as I think they were too, when the border patrol dropped the barrier behind us, separating us with the weight of the Iron Curtain.

Two years later, Elvira became another member of my extended family whose presence in the States I promoted and/or financed. Four years later, she and her family were refugees from Czechoslovakia and went on to Israel with my enthusiastic moral and financial support. Her frantic telephone call from Vienna came to us in Pittsburgh during the time her brother Pali from Prague was our houseguest. Pali, an old-time socialist, had taken Dubcek's fall very much to heart. He was also worried about his sister's status and her future in Israel. Perhaps he assessed the situation a bit too pessimistically. For by now he has visited her in Israel, and she has been abroad once, rendezvousing with him in Stockholm. Elvira and her husband receive pension payments from the West German government. Her children are well established in Jerusalem, each in his/her profession. They are already planning their sabbatical in the United States, in two years' time.

During the train ride from Vienna to Budapest I was a bundle of nerves in anticipation. Suddenly, my view of The River of my childhood mingled with flashes of the Ohio in Pittsburgh. And as Harold and I crossed over the bridge to Pest, I was shocked to see how the mighty Danube had shrunk in width. We arrived at the Eastern Terminal incognito and, for all practical purposes, as if I were a first-time tourist. Knowledge of the language and my childhood in Hungary, however, provided an instant key to unlocking the mysteries total strangers with no connections may have upon first encounter. The landmarks of my earliest years were an immediate "must" on my program. I visited the apartment I was born in, the *gymnazium* I had attended, and Margit Island, where I had spent so many happy times. For refreshments and iced café and *patisserie,* I sat in the Vig Café and in the famous Gerbaud, now named after a revolutionary poet. I walked along every block and past every reminder of my childhood. I also went to see some of the tourist attractions and even hired a cab to drive me around for an hour's aimless wandering. I was distressed to see some streets and squares renamed in honor of heroes of Communism: Lenin Boulevard, Engels Lane, Marx Square, Avenue of the Peoples Republic, Rosenberg Couple (Ethel and Julius) Street. At the same time, I was beaming with pride to be able to share with Harold the rediscovery of my physical roots.

The more I came into contact with the geography and the culture of the city, the more confirmed I became in my decision not to look up classmates or distant relatives; in Vienna, I had struggled with this thought a great deal, weighing all the considerations pro and contra. Alternately I was curious and anxious to renew contacts so long ago broken—and felt callous and heartless in rejecting the idea.

After meeting Elvira, did I really need to seek out persons whose stories could only further depress me? In my self-analysis, I went the path of feeling guilty for being spared their fate and selfish for not willingly exposing myself to a confrontation. I also knew my emotional limits. Israeli relatives and now newly found cousins in Czechoslovakia had involved me enough, financially as well as emotionally. I was determined to enjoy my present and future Budapest visits without personal entanglements with the past. Although I continue to send semiannual remittances to a distant relative, I keep this connection on a strictly impersonal level. Consequent visits to my native city were enhanced by the Israeli diplomtic presence in the person of Guszti from Jerusalem, and by contacts with Klari's in-laws, with Vera's sister and with Jancsi, a friend whom I met other times in Vienna and London.

One very special occasion in Budapest was shared with my

daughter Ellen, who was on her way home from her (high school) junior summer and semester in Israel. She and I met in Vienna first, enjoying a marvelous holiday in each other's company. There, by prearrangement, she took a part of her College Board examinations. Also, on an impulse, we saw *Carmen* in the recently refurbished Opera House. It was my special pleasure then to escort Ellie myself to Budapest and show her around. We "did" all the sights, including my birthplace and Margit Island. We attended a performance of the famous Puppet Theater and saw an exquisitely danced *Nutcracker Suite*. I introduced her to the aromatic taste sensation still lingering among my fondest recollections: the fresh-roasted chestnut. These were prepared on little portable ovens that glowed with red-hot coals, in innumerable sidewalk locations, and were dispensed in brown paper twisted into cone-shaped bags. Just as I had remembered them from my childhood.

A few years later, Klari and Bill and Harold and I were in Budapest at the same time. Cousin Pali from Prague also being on hand, and the three of them knowing every one of the city's celebrated spas and equally superb restaurants, this visit was a particularly enjoyable one.

Chapter 12

Penthouse

Big house and big grounds were no longer a practical setting for my emptying nest. After children went away to college, judging from examples around us, they were not likely to come back to live in Pittsburgh. The restless migration of the young was already in full swing. Our oldest son was married by then and was settling down elsewhere. Even if the others did return to Pittsburgh after completing their studies, they would prefer to set up their own households—the popular formula. Our own travel pattern was bound to continue. Nor were my responsibilities for the house and garden lessening, and household help was difficult to keep. With our daughter about to leave Pittsburgh to attend university, I decided that this was the right moment to move into an apartment. I wanted to give up flights of stairs before I was unable to climb them.

An attractive alternative presented itself—and we took it: a spacious double penthouse (two three-bedroom units) in a new high-rise building, the only one around. Here we would have rooms for ourselves, for Father, for our youngest son then attending the University of Pittsburgh, and for our daughter to keep until she should marry. A double rooftop terrace, which we landscaped, provided additional possibilities for entertaining. It gave a marvelous unobstructed view over our city's Golden

Triangle and its environs, with a radius of some five miles on a clear day. This view included the smokestacks of the steel mills along the rivers as well as the green flanks of the Allegheny Mountains to the east. All this and the convenience of apartment living in absolute privacy! Here was a proposition I could not resist. Thus, for six years Maxon Towers provided the ideal transition from the Golden Age of Family to the Empty Nest.

There were many pleasant and exciting family events during the penthouse years. The children continued to return home for the holidays, secular and religious, their academic obligations permitting, if sometimes for only a day and a night. Golden Age of Family was still operative; in its winddown we delighted in every occasion that signaled the children's presence with us and together with each other. These years also included college graduations, graduate studies, first jobs and, for all of the children, marriage.

Eddie's and Ellie's weddings were home based and involved me in much planning and exciting arrangements. Mother's and daughter's dream wedding, Ellie's was a traditional ceremony with some enchanting original touches devised by the young couple. One of these was the music played by a string trio (Pittsburgh Symphony friends) before and after the ceremony: selections from Mozart and Haydn. The bride's brother, Eddie, then a rabbinical student, assisted in the service. Our rooftop and our large apartment lent themselves beautifully to prewedding festivities. One additional Ruttenberg wedding reception took place here, that of our niece Merle, for whom I was happy to hold an extended family celebration. By then we had three grandchildren; the occasional homecomings of all the children and of the three little ones were especially welcome.

For my father's ninetieth birthday, I invited about ninety guests including his New York and Chicago nieces and nephews. Father was his alert self and promised Jack, the oldest among them, to return the visit by attending Jack's ninetieth birthday party. I also arranged a surprise appearance by Father's old buddy from Westinghouse days, a long-time New Yorker. Together with the children, other relatives, and friends, Father was a truly beautiful excuse for a memorable celebration.

Two of the many social events held in the penthouse were connected with art. One took place the weekend the new Temple Sinai sanctuary was dedicated. As we had commissioned many of the art works and had been consulted on some others, it was our special pleasure to entertain the two artists most involved, Chaim Gross and Naftali Bezem. Gross is the American sculptor, watercolorist and lithographer who created the seven-foot Menorahs (candelabra) in and in front of Temple Sinai. Bezem is the Israeli painter and sculptor who designed the stained-glass window over the altar, the window I "supervised" from its manufacture in an Israeli workshop to its installation.

The other art affair was in connection with the 1967 Carnegie International Exhibition of Paintings and Sculpture, a prestigious art event that has been held regularly in Pittsburgh ever since 1896. In 1967, one of our Israeli artists was represented by a stunning abstract *Seascape,* and our dear friend Pittsburgher Samuel Rosenberg by a large brilliant *Composition.* Without a moment of hesitation, we bought both works on preview night. In addition, Pablo Serrano, one the Spanish artists whom we had visited in Cuenca, had his sculpture *Man with Door* in the show and was in Pittsburgh for the occasion, as was Juano Mordo, Madrid's foremost art dealer. Our acquisitions and the presence of Serrano and Mordo among our guests added an extra glow to the festivities.

My social horizon has been constantly expanding. During the Golden Age of Family, overseas travel added also an international dimension to it. My extracurricular interests, our art involvements and Harold's business, Israel and literary activities[16] further widened it. By the time we moved into the penthouse, Harold and I had great need for a private secretary: he would not conduct his personal affairs through his corporate office, even though it was a private company and he was the majority stockholder.

Freda Leff, who had served as secretary of Temple Sinai for twenty-one years, was by chance then available. She and I had become personal friends through the many Sinai projects we had in common, and so our new relationship was off to a propitious start.

Harold took over one of the penthouse living-dining area

rooms for his studio/office and library. Freda was installed in her own office in the adjacent smaller room; until recently, she had her own office space in our present home as well. In addition to helping with our personal and community activities, Freda was kind enough to carry responsibility for Father's welfare—he was then in failing health—during my absences from home. Her many courtesies and acts of kindness towards him until the end are deeply appreciated.

Freda continued as our full-time personal secretary until 1973, when we elected voting machines to be the major fact of our business life. She then became a full-time secretary in the Pittsburgh executive office of the AVM Corporation, a mini-conglomerate whose management Harold took over when the firm was in financial difficulties. As Chairman, President and Chief Executive Officer and largest stockholder (with me), he has since turned the company around.

To my good fortune, Freda is willing to continue to work for me outside office hours. Currently there are even more events and social affairs held at home than there were in the penthouse. Sending out invitations (her calligraphy is beyond compare!), arranging for refreshments, working out time-tables and countless other details are chores with which Freda has had much experience. Also being a free-lance party and wedding consultant, she brings many skills to her job. Tactful in personal dealings but direct when indicated, she attends to her assignments with efficiency and much understanding. With Father (then in his eighties) living with us, with children and grandchildren still returning for occasional visits and with two extensive greeting card mailings a year, Freda in her office at our home and outside office hours has provided a much-needed continuity in our private lives. She still does.

During our shopping cart days, overlapping Aylesboro and the penthouse, we had, besides overseas travel, one other fringe benefit: holidays on Gull Lake, a picturesque nature reserve area adjacent to Battle Creek, Michigan, where the company was headquartered. For four summers in a row (1964-68) I kept house on the lake. We had visits from children, relatives and friends during the two-or-three-week periods we stayed there. Charlie's wedding took place on the front lawn bordering the lake, under lovely low trees forming a natural wedding canopy. We also maintained a Ruttenberg Navy consisting of a flat-bottomed pontoon boat, a canoe and a pedalo. To help me with housekeeping, I invited Lilly, a former employee, to live with us; her domestic talents were more than matched by her skills at fishing. From Gull Lake we flew to Washington, D.C., in a private plane to witness President Johnson's swearing in of my brother-in-law Stanley as Assistant Secretary of Labor. When not in Pittsburgh or at Gull Lake or in Israel, Harold and I sold shopping carts in Europe and Japan.

Before my brief spell as an English theme reader, my interest in writing was confined to college term papers, reports, minutes of meetings and letters. That is, if one does not count: notes to the milkman, lists of things to pack for camp, memos on household shopping, reminders on what to discuss with teacher, pediatrician and plumber. I am a compulsive list maker. I have always been a conscientious letter writer: to those who are away from home and conversely, to those whom I leave at home; to friends as well. Whenever I have new and interesting things to write home about, my letters become minitravelogues, generously punctuated with comments and observations.

From straight reporting I branched out into writing about unusual personal experiences. My vivid accounts of our Seder in Saigon (1960) and of my nightmarish twenty-seven hours flight from Chicago to Pittsburgh in an April 2 blizzard (1975) are early and recent examples, respectively, of my writing efforts. Since the early sixties, several of my reports and book reviews have appeared in the local Jewish press; and I don't mind admitting that seeing my thoughts and by-line in print gives me a pleasant feeling. My articles, printed or not, have become popular among the small circle of friends to whom they are sent. When there is a long pause between articles, some persons on my basic mailing list (children are always included) actually register continued interest in my writings. This I find most flattering.

I hoped someday to write something for a wider audience. This occasion occurred under most trying circumstances: the Yom Kippur War, about which I wrote as a witness to it and as a volunteer driver of soldiers on leave to and from their army posts. Marcia Ripp joined me on this exciting venture of three weeks, and she and I wrote articles for the *Pittsburgh Post-Gazette*, most of which were published. I expanded these reports of my experiences on the road to Jericho into "A Volunteer in Jerusalem, '73," a sixty-three-page monograph that I distributed among family, friends, acquaintances and business associates.

My last two book reviews in the *Jewish Chronicle* were of Saul Bellow's *To Jerusalem and Back* (jointly with Harold, December 16, 1976) and of *For Jerusalem—A Life by Teddy Kollek* (June 8, 1978). I was especially interested in the former because I had spent a stimulating evening with Bellow at AviHai's home during the author's stay in Jerusalem as the city's VIP guest. Bellow is a forceful conversationalist and a skilled raconteur of Yiddish stories as well as of personal anecdotes. He is the only Nobel Prize winner I have ever met (not counting Menachem Begin, 1978 Peace Prize corecipient, to whom I was recently introduced by a mutual friend). I also took special delight in reading and reviewing Kollek's book because of my personal connection with the man and because of my interest in his historical overview as well as in some of his current pet projects in behalf of Jerusalem.

I have been bitten by the writing bug. I sometimes go on a holiday carrying my portable typewriter just in case I might be tempted. In the typing of this story of my life, I have shuttled between a baby Hermes and an Olympia in the miniflat and my new Olivetti at Fifth Avenue. In the course of writing it (the most concentration I have ever practiced in this field) I have come to the conclusion that there are many things to write about (perhaps nothing should ever be ruled out); but also that some things, having been written, should never see the light of day. A valuable lesson, I believe.

My involvement with Israeli cousins took some very personal dimensions in three special situations. One concerned Dafna Aba and her two daughters, who lived in Pittsburgh in 1964–66. (She later remarried and is now Dafna Weinholtz.) Father had by then moved in with us, and so Dafna had the garage apartment for her own use. Her presence in our midst was a happy experience for me and my family and a very successful one for her. She is a talented teacher and was well liked both by her kindergarten classes and by her adult students, whom she taught Hebrew. She made many friends and greatly improved her English. Along with all the pluses there were, however, some trying instances that pointed up the nature of one's responsibility undertaken in someone's behalf.

When Dafna returned to Israel and started a new and better life for herself and her children, we became interested in Yochanan Stern's dreams and ambitions. The son of another cousin and a fine young man of twenty-eight, Yochanan was in need of American industrial experience. I therefore busied myself with his case. The offer of a job at Harold's United Steel and Wire Company in Battle Creek provided the legal basis for his coming. To enable him to earn a living, Yochanan had to arrive in America as an immigrant; we on our part had to show evidence that the company needed his skill and could not find anyone in the general vicinity qualified to fill the job. He was a certificated toolmaker.

Yochanan's nearness to us in America (1969–72) coincided with a period in our lives when all our children were for the first time away from home. Yochanan, his wife, Dena, and two children were sociable, devoted and cooperative; whenever we were together, the young Israelis were a lively and welcome addition to our shrinking family at home.

During the three and a quarter years that he spent in America, Yochanan learned to be a competent middle-management person. He also studied English and economics at a community college and finished a practical course of studies at a technical institute, earning an associate degree in production engineering. Yochanan and his family, increased by one little Yankee and another little sabra, are today in Jerusalem better off than they would have been without their American experience.

At ten years of age, Dorit Shavit, cousin Guszti's daughter, was my Ellie's companion in an Israeli camp, Haddasim, near Natanya. Throughout their teens, the girls continued a close friendship and were able to meet in person in Israel and even once in Vienna. When I planned Ellie's wedding, I wished to add something special to the arrangements. So, although Dorit was still serving in the Israeli Army, I managed her flight into Pittsburgh on a six weeks' leave to the complete surprise and delight of the bride and all the wedding party. I was also responsible for Dorit's return to us for two years of studies (1973–75) at the University of Pittsburgh. Personable, kind and a good companion, she lived at 5100 Fifth Avenue with us (our home after the penthouse). She was a welcome member of our family, being at the end a bit of a crutch for me in my shock at finding the nest empty. This too was a happy experience for me, and I can only presume that for Dorit, too, her Pittsburgh interlude was rewarding and enriching.

Chapter 13

Travel Abroad

Travel and art collecting, both of which had their start during the Aylesboro period, are still active elements in my life. On both subjects, I have given talks over the years; and art to this day occasionally forms the focus around which there is a gathering in my home.

Travel really began for us in the mid-fifties. At that time, if you already belonged to a country club and had your second postwar big car, you went on to a patio, an impressive game room doubling as an entertainment center, or travel abroad. We already had our Cadillac, we preferred to remain unclubbed, and Harold liked to sit and rock on the front porch. However, I took Harold's reluctance to get off the porch lightly and persisted in pointing out the obvious benefits and advantages of foreign travel. Such momentous decisions we were used to. Several years before, when neighbors were competing for their first postwar Cadillac, we had bought our Steinway baby grand piano. Now, as we were both approaching forty, I campaigned for a trip abroad. We were fortunate in that Stardrill Keystone Drilling Company (which Harold headed as President, Chairman of the Board and Chief Executive Officer from 1951 through 1959) was a worldwide business, water well drilling machines of all sizes and models being familiar landmarks everywhere in the Americas and on other continents as well. For the good of the company, therefore, and armed with contacts in government and business offices, we set out on an ambitious overseas selling assignment. Our first trip abroad (July–August, 1954) hit the high points that any tourist would envy and included Israel as well.

I love sightseeing. Monuments and museums, caves and castles, excavations of the past and constructions for the future— all have a fascination for me. I am interested, and I am curious. Though my foreign journeys only began when I was forty, I hope that, given good health and the means to do it, my travel will continue for years to come. Through business, through private referrals and lately through art, I have had personal contacts nearly everywhere I went. I still do. In fact, the folks I have met and the several friends I have gained are as much a benefit as the sightseeing itself.

Sr. Fiero (devilish older man, industrial empire builder) was our business contact in Spain; Mr. Kazis (all business and no sense of humor) in Greece. Adil Gabay (a cosmopolitan intellectual, a proud Jew and a Freemason) was our man in Istanbul and Switzerland; Fritz Denes (a successful Hungarian transplant in Turkey) showed us Kemal Ataturk's creation, Ankara. With the Lundbergs (lovable and naturally sociable) we did Stockholm, their native city, and Monaco where they live; their residence in Monte Carlo is our address in Europe. Our sales agents were responsible for us in the South American capitals and in the Far East. Company presidents and chief engineers awaited us at airports; flowers and fruit baskets greeted us in our hotel rooms. Commercial attachés of the United States embassies and cabinet ministers took an interest in our program. Being received in private homes, accompanied on shopping sprees and taken to entertainment places played a major role in my exposure to other countries and other cultures. In addition, Harold and I made many excursions by ourselves, spending much time in private explorations of our own. Everywhere, however, there were genial hosts, who with their kind gestures made our visits unforgettable and offered many possibilities not usually available to the mere tourist.

On my first trip abroad, we met Carlos Boyer, a cultured man our own age, a linguist of note and a bon vivant. He was engaged by our business associates to devote nearly full time to assisting us during our stay in Madrid, and he was also the official interpreter in all business negotiations. Carlos, with impeccable European manners and sympathico Mediterranean character, was at our beck and call any hour of the day and evening, which in Spain most often extends into the night. A lawyer by profession, whose practice was hindered by his having been a Loyalist, he was also an impressario and an art connoisseur. During the intervening years we have enjoyed each other's company on many excursions in Spain, notably to Cordoba, Granada and Cuenca.[17] I also met him once in Rome and once in Madrid. We keep in touch.

We did a superb job of taking advantage of American Point Four money available to foreign governments in their development schemes and returned from our first trip abroad after a grueling and exciting nine weeks with absolute success. We had thus embarked on an irreversible path of foreign travel, and the sick company Harold had acquired three years earlier was suddenly on the upswing. Subsequent trips in its behalf resulted in a phenomenal increase in its profitability. Point Four was a handy vehicle for selling drilling machines, thus helping in the development of water resources in over fifty countries on three continents. Under Stardrill Keystone Drilling Machine auspices, we traveled abroad ten times in six years, and through our contacts and hosts we enjoyed a personalized and in-depth exposure to the sites, sounds and smells of Europe, South America and the Orient.

My role on both the business and accompanying social levels has always been inseparable from Harold's. In fact, I am confident that innumerable times my sociability and participation in extraoffice meetings with our hosts made the difference that resulted in a transaction. I recall that on one occasion, in a charming country tavern on the way to Sunyon, there was a serious language barrier between us and our business associates. My French didn't carry us past menus, the climate and our itinerary. Their English was even more elementary. So in a moment of desperation, I devised a word game that our Greek hosts and we could play to keep congeniality afloat. It was practically a solo performance of my own, however, as I recited all the words in English and French that I could think of that derived from Greek, complementing them with simple English and elaborate pantomime: from *theater* and *cinema* to *crystal* and *prophet;* from *tele*'s, *epi*'s and *philo*'s to *'graphs* and *'ologies*. The Greeks were as astounded as they were flattered, and I was grateful to Mr. Webster and to my father's influence. One of the most exhausting social events of my "business" career proved to be a resounding success.

In Paris, we viewed Chagall's *Jerusalem Windows* before they were shown in New York and installed in the Hadassah Hospital in Jerusalem. We rummaged through all the stalls on the left bank of the Seine looking for old etchings and engravings of city views and ancient maps. We visited many of the lesser-known museums in the capitals of Europe and explored most of them in southern France. (The Louvre, Prado, Tate and British Museums we periodically revisit.) We heard opera in Paris, Vienna, Milan, Budapest; and enjoyed plays and concerts in London and Budapest.

I refused Harold's offer of a mink coat in Stockholm (I wasn't ready for it then). I swam in the refreshing waters of the Marmara Sea (Istanbul), of Lake Lugano, and of the Mediterranean as guest of the Le Club Sportif of Monte Carlo. In Madrid, I witnessed (sometime with horror) a bullfight with commentary by our Spanish companion, Carlos; and toured Rome by night— as the Romans do—in the company of our Italian business partners. As houseguests of Finland's soft-drink king, we participated in the ritual of the sauna—where it is indigenous to the culture. In order to make the last commercial flight to Budapest, we hired a private plane in Munich to get us to Vienna on time, thus getting a low-flying view of the picturesque panorama of verdant forests, storybook castles and neat little towns along the bends of the Danube.

My last business trip under drilling machine auspices was one around the world in 1960. Except for a month's visit six years later in Japan (in the path of our rolling shopping carts), it provided my most intensive acquaintance with the Orient. The trip continued through India to Israel and home via Europe. We spent a memorable Seder in Saigon at a time when the American military mission was still operating in low profile. We stood on the road to Mandalay. We made a pilgrimage to the Taj Mahal in the moonlight and there awaited the sunrise. A monument of love of a man for a woman, Taj Mahal is where Harold and I had one of the most serious disagreements of our married life. We had a private audience with Prime Minister Tengku Abdul Rahman of Malaysia, with whom we discussed the economy and the demographic problems of his country ("the Chinese multiply at too fast a rate," he maintained).

Accompanied by our Indian hostess (partner in the export/ import company we were dealing with), we bought exquisite saris and, on our own, three Persian tapestries (Moses, Aaron and a large silk ark cover) between planes in Teheran. In the company of our Thai business associates, we visited most of Bangkok's temples and cruised some of its many canals—actually twice. Another agent courting us for our business also felt obliged to give us the full tour; we on the other hand also felt obliged to accept. We witnessed the coming-of-age ceremony for a boy of the Parsi community in Karachi. In Singapore and Delhi, we were entertained in private clubs, heritage of the English colonial establishment; we toured a Pakistani village where the only other white woman before me had been Eleanor Roosevelt. We bought ivory, Thai silk, Burmese teak, Philippine pina shirts, and all of Singapore's duty-free Jensen silver. We sat on a bench in Kipling's favorite park in Lahore. In Calcutta, we visited a Jewish girls' school, heard a lecture on anthropology and walked over sleeping bodies on the sidewalk. We arrived everywhere just ahead of the monsoon.

Shopping carts and wire products took us to Japan in 1966. In Tokyo, I found the mentality of the Japanese puzzling and the hustle and bustle overwhelming. We looked into a few art galleries and saw the fabulous collection of paintings from the

Hermitage, then on tour from Leningrad. We visited both the Western and the native museums and were taken by our Japanese hosts to be entertained by their favorite geisha girls. We rode in the superspeedy luxury train to and from Kyoto, where we spent two days visiting temples, admiring the scenery, and getting acquainted with an English couple whose name within a few years became well known in intellectual circles everywhere.

We had a mutual friend in another Englishman, physicist/philosopher Lancelot Law Whyte, who had been a houseguest of ours on several occasions. Jacob Bronowsky was then gathering material for and in the midst of writing his book *The Ascent of Man* and talked freely to us about his work; he was totally engrossed in it. We found him stimulating company. Several years later, we enjoyed reading the book and viewing the television series based on it with an extra measure of understanding because of our personal encounter in Japan.

Chapter 14

Israel

The very first time I came to Israel I boarded the plane at Istanbul. I was excited for two good reasons: curiosity about the country and anticipation of meeting members of my extended family, some for the first time. The years and our totally different life experiences over almost three decades vanished upon first sight, and we took to each other instantly. Whether my growing interest over the succeeding years in Israel's fate added an aura of importance to my Israeli family or they in turn caused me to become more deeply involved remains a moot question. In any case, it is certain that family ties have provided an added dimension to my Israeli experience and the life I lead as a part-time Yerushalmi (Jerusalemite).

In 1954 I had three first cousins and an aunt in Jerusalem whom I remembered from my childhood. Another aunt and three more cousins came later. Today, with children, grandchildren and great-grandchildren as well as assorted spouses—and through natural attrition—the clan numbers over forty. After a week of touring and attending to our business duties, Harold and I drove into Jerusalem. When, upon arrival in the country, I telephoned my aunt, I learned precisely when and where we would meet. What I could not forecast was the emotional impact our reunion would have on all of us.

Their hospitality was incomparable. They had saved up ration coupons for weeks in order to provide us with superb meals and tempting snacks—precious coffee flowed freely—during our whirlwind four days in Jerusalem. Our festive dinner party at the King David Hotel for the whole family on the eve of our departure wasn't even in the same league with the home-cooked Hungarian cuisine with which they feted us.

The two languages among us were, and for the most part still are, Hungarian, the mother tongue of all of my generation (whether they were born in Hungary, Czechoslovakia or Rumania), and English. They all speak Hebrew, some better than others. Nearly everyone of the clan also speaks English, some better than others. My own facility in Hungarian made a miraculous comeback when I renewed relationships on my first visit in Israel. The more time I have spent there since, the more fluent my native language has become. I think in English, but the little arithmetic I am obliged to perform in my daily life I do best in Hungarian. When I am deeply troubled or in sudden shock, my expletives are Hungarian—though English gets equal billing in all my dreams.

Water well drilling took us back to Israel several more times; on each occasion we were exposed to new sites and new experiences. The King David Hotel became a home away from home, though before 1967, like most tourists, we spent more time headquartering in Tel Aviv than in Jerusalem. The younger members of the clan went with us occasionally on sightseeing tours, but cousin Guszti became my chief guide and escort on foot, by rental car and even as I perched on his Vespa motor scooter; later in his 404 Peugeot. A veteran of the Jewish Brigade (World War II) and an old time Israeli, Guszti holds a sensitive government post. Among all my family he is one especially dear to me.

Immediately following the Six Day War, Harold arranged for the Israel Aircraft Industries to acquire the Jet Commander business from the Rockwell enterprises. In the fall of 1967, Harold and I helped to bring the Rockwell Jet Commander plane into Israel. We urged Colonel Rockwell, then seventy-five, to use this business occasion for his first visit to Israel. When he agreed, we knew that protocol would call for numerous events that a mere sale of a patent or a know-how agreement would not command. It was thus in the midst of some fuss and formality (low-key that they were) that I stepped out of the elegantly outfitted Jet Commander Executive plane we had boarded in Nice, accompanying the Colonel, his wife, Harold, and an Israel government liaison official.

We flew over the West Bank, circled over reunited Jerusalem in a DC-3 parachutists' plane and landed in East Jerusalem's Kalandria Airport, which was a "first" in nineteen years for an Israeli plane. Staff persons from Military Industries, the Commerce Ministry and the Prime Minister's Office were attached to our party for all conferences and the much-too-quick sightseeing. An official banquet was held toasting the American giant of industry and in anticipation of great financial and prestige advantages accruing to Israel as a result of the Jet Commander deal. We also called on Prime Minister Levi Eshkol and went to the home of then Commerce and Industry Minister Ze'ev Sharef,[18] one of the early State founders, for a working luncheon meeting. Whether he is in or out of government and with whatever title, Sharef remains a good friend of ours.

Once, at a private dinner at the Sharefs' home, Golda Meir and we were the only guests. What a unique opportunity to discover a famous personality behind the headlines, clichés and public facade! I was immensely impressed by Golda's inner strength, dedication and warmth; her presence was magnetic. She was dressed somewhat less severely than usually portrayed; the soft neckline rendered her uncommon facial features most appealing. Her eyes sparkled as she and our hosts reminisced about their and the country's early days. Their relationships to fellow founders of the State and to some of the diaspora Jewish leadership she referred to in affectionate but realistic terms. She urged Harold to explore industrial possibilities in her daughter's kibbutz, Revivim, deep in the heart of the Negev. This we did shortly afterwards, but unfortunately nothing tangible came out of Harold's proposals.

Soon after the Jet Commander deal, when Ze'ev Sharef and his wife Henya came to America on official business, I flew to New York to help her do some shopping for their family. Her friendship was dear to me, and when she died she left a void in my Jerusalem life. Ze'ev lives alone in his villa with a multilevel garden that overlooks Yad V'Shem[19] and a magnificent panorama. He entertains frequently with easy informality; his surprise seventieth-birthday party, to which his children invited me, was an eloquent testimony to the respect and love of his family and of his friends.

This relationship is just one of many that have established personal ties for me in the social life of Jerusalem. I am also aware of the special, sometimes even rare, opportunities Harold's professional activities and our art involvements have provided for us through the years. In citing a few instances of personalized tours or events, I express my deepest gratitude to all who have made my association with Israel meaningful. To all whose friendship I enjoy. To all whose presence there ensures my constant return.

Among the rock formations in the S'dom area, deep water well drilling back in 1960 was a great promise as yet unfulfilled. Harold and his geologist/master driller alerted our business associate, David Uriely, to this possibility by explaining the presence of hydraulic pressure arising from higher levels of underground water storage. Before the Six Day War this spot bordering on Jordan was almost inaccessible. One could reach the heights and depths of this rugged terrain only by jeep, on foot, or on the back of a mule. S'dom, the Dead Sea resort, was then no more than a cluster of huts without any amenities. After seeing the Dead Sea from behind Lot's wife turned to salt, (a rock formation), I was delighted to reach it for a coffee break. S'dom accommodations of today are a far cry from those of pre-1967. This highly developed seat (one of several) of Israel's spa industry now lures seekers of health from abroad to its therapeutic waters, up-to-date medical facilities and chic hotels.

During the months immediately after the Six Day War in 1967, Hebron was one of the most explosive locations in the administered areas. Whenever tour buses could go there at all, tourists stopped only in the well-patrolled portions of the town: the sole

Jewish café and gift shop and the Machpela (the burial place of Abraham, Isaac and Jacob; Sarah, Rebecca and Leah). It was enough for visitors to get a mere glimpse of this ancient city with its recent history written in blood, without exposing them to danger. Harold and I were taken on a personal tour of Hebron by Joshua Cohen, then David Ben-Gurion's bodyguard, and Nachman Fein, our Histadrut friend, who made the arrangements. Leading a couple of armed men, Joshua escorted us through the Arab *suk* ("market") and the old Jewish cemetery. Strangely, I was quite oblivious to the unusual precautions taken; and it wasn't until, in my curiosity, I tried to stray from our little party that I became aware of my gun-toting companions. I was greatly impressed by the tradition that claims the burial places of the patriarchs and matriarchs but somewhat less so by their present appearance. I was also moved by the references to biblical passages at many places in and around Hebron, all of which I followed in the English text as soon as Joshua and Nachman found them in the Hebrew Scriptures.

One of the many special experiences that Guszti assisted in realizing for me in the early years was attendance at one of the sessions of the trial of Adolf Eichman. The atmosphere was tense in Jerusalem in July, 1961, as the eyes of the world were on the courtroom in *Beit Ha-Am* ("House of the People").

When on my birthday in May, 1960, we flew from Lod to Rome on the same plane with a prominent VIP, Abba Eban, I thought that was exciting enough. What I didn't know was the significance of the plane. It so happened that, after discharging passengers in Rome, the plane flew on to Buenos Aires where Eban represented Israel at the celebration of 150 years of Argentinian independence. Two days later, the world electrified to learn of Eichman's capture in Argentina; he was spirited onto this same plane and flown to Israel to face trial.

Eichman, medium sized, insignificant looking, with receding hair and ill-fitting false teeth, was questioned in a glass booth in Beit Ha-Am. The Nazi officer in charge of the extermination of the Jews in Europe, he spoke on the hideous crime with which he was charged. Journalists and reporters, survivors and other middle-aged and elderly people, immigrants from Europe and a sprinkling of old-time Israelis—these were the immediate audience to which the trial directed itself. In the larger sense, the whole world was the audience. The three judges, the prosecutor and defender, and a team of translators completed the awesome drama to which I was a witness. Beit Ha-Am was surrounded by high fences and was guarded from roof to cellar by heavily armed police. In the front courtyard was a row of wooden barracks in which we were frisked before we were allowed in. This was indeed a most extraordinary occasion; I am forever grateful to Guszti for making my admission possible.

The Israeli kibbutz has fascinated behavioral scientists ever since it originally appeared as a communal agricultural settlement. In its evolution, it has been the testing ground for various types of political Zionism combined with several shades of socialism. My earliest recollection of kibbutzim is of Ein Dor in the Galilee; this is where Eddie spent the summer of 1965 picking pears and learning more Hebrew. In 1968, when we were showing Lon Kight,[20] a vice-president of Rockwell, around the country, we visited Affikim together. This was where the Military Industries directed the guide to take us and where by chance he had family. We were given an extensive tour of the Affikim plywood factory and a lecture on its role in the economy. We were also dinner guests at the kibbutz. Affikim, situated on the southern shore of Lake Kinneret, is one of the largest kibbutzim in the country. I have also attended a family wedding celebration there.

We were on one occasion guests in Golda Meir's daughter's kibbutz. We went to Revivim for a combination of social and "business" reasons: it was upon Golda's suggestion that we were invited to advise Revivim leaders in regard to the settlement's industrial development. Another kibbutz in the Negev, famous for one of its founders, David Ben-Gurion, is where we visited in 1970. The former prime minister, resigned from active political life a second time, had retired to his desert home to finish his years in quiet study and writing. Out of government, Ben-Gurion was still a controversial though respected voice of his country. Our escort on this excursion was Joshua Cohen, an old-time

member of Ben-Gurion's security guard, who had also taken us to
Hebron. No hired guide, he was doing us a favor, as a kind ac-
commodation also for a mutual friend. We visited a site where a
young sculptor envisioned an elaborate sculpture field. Then,
after a brief stop at the nearby institute of the same name, where
the sculptor had his studio, we arrived at Kibbutz S'de Boker in
mid-afternoon.

I had the distinct feeling of being in close proximity to a great
personality. While I had no excuse nor courage to call on Ben-
Gurion in his home, I did at least share a Shabat supper with him.
When he strolled into the dining hall, relaxed and smiling and
dressed for Shabat with a necktie on, there was not a stir among
his fellow kibbutzniks; only for me was this an extraordinary happening, to see and feel this man's presence in a personal, homelike setting, completely outside officialdom. The tie was in con-
tradiction to the widely held notion that Ben Gurion never wore
one, except of course at international and state occasions, when
he referred to dress-up and formal suits as his "working clothes."
The few times I have seen him in large gatherings and all the
miles of words I have read about him no way prepared me for the
excitement of this close-range encounter in the flesh, including an
informal introduction by Joshua on our way out of the dining hall.

Celebration of Seder night can be something of a dilemma.
Shall I accept the first invitation that comes along? From family
or a friend? In any case, someone's feelings may be hurt. The
year we were invited to Hatzerim, just outside Beersheba, our
problem was resolved in a most delightful way; for a kibbutz
Seder is not to be missed if you have never been to one. Without
hesitation we accepted their invitation to the observance and had a
great time as guests of Aharon Yadlin, always prominent in Labor
party affairs and later Minister of Education and Culture in
Golda's and Rabin's cabinets. We spent several leisurely hours
with the Yadlins in their house and walking about the grounds,
and later participated in the communal Seder that evening.

The nonreligious kibbutzim not only celebrate the historical
theme of the Passover[21] holiday but especially highlight the agricultural aspect of the festival. This was so in Hatzerim. Young

girls in flowing white gowns with floral wreaths on their heads and carrying wicker baskets, filled with early spring fruits and vegetables, floated by before us. This symbolized the harvesting of the first barley in ancient days in the land of Israel. This bit of pageantry was one of several interesting touches that emphasized the seasonal background (planting to harvest) of the festival without eliminating its religious/historical meaning, as related in the Haggadah. The narration (literal meaning of the word) for the Seder is based on the story of Exodus. The singing by the kibbutz choir and the participation of all members in song and ritual was most impressive; the festive meal was absolutely superb.

I have a standing invitation to Gevi'im, home of Tzippy, Sharef's daughter. I have already taken her up on it once, with Klari. We spent a wonderful day and night with Tzippy and her husband in their kibbutz. They vacated their cozy two-room flat for our comfort. A most hospitable gesture! I was particularly interested in the kibbutz philosophy of bringing up children. Gevi'im had started out with a completely communal system: children of various age groups, from birth on, were looked after and cared for in children's houses, by staff especially trained to do so. At the time we visited Gevi'im, a change in child-rearing methods had just recently been voted in. The kibbutz was at this time gradually putting into effect the "new" system of letting children live with their parents. This meant, among other things, that new housing would be built to accommodate born-again families. There was a flurry of excitement among the younger members in anticipation of new challenges and for them as yet undefined responsibilities.

I am always curious about any industrial enterprise that may be a basis of a kibbutz economy. In Gevi'im I was astonished to learn that a popular musical instrument, one that each of my children plays well, was being produced here, for domestic needs as well as for export. It is in fact the best Israeli-made recorder, as fine an instrument as made anywhere. I enjoyed the complete tour of the production facilities as well as the packaging and shipping departments. I promptly bought ten recorders in several ranges at the retail price, less a small discount, for the grandchildren. I can't think of a sweeter sound to bring a fond recall of a memorable kibbutz visit someday when my grandchildren too will play recorders.

Mishmar HaEmek is the only other kibbutz where I spent a day and a night as guest of a member. Hadassah Samuel and I arrived from Rosh Pina where we had been visiting with my friend, Carol Elias.[22] Edwin Samuel's niece Yaela and her husband were our hosts, and they couldn't do enough for their favorite aunt and me. They were extremely hospitable, even giving up their bedroom and moving in with friends in order for us to have two separate rooms to sleep in. What I especially enjoyed besides their company were Yaela's enthusiastic views on the hard-line socialist orientation of the kibbutz.

In both Gevi'im and Mishmar HaEmek, I was able to observe something of family life, especially the ways parents and children relate to each other and how children manage their own lives in their homes. I was delighted to see how much warmth and dedication parents brought to the going-to-bed ritual; and how a problem-free time of togetherness was spent for at least two hours in the family circle every afternoon and sometimes even including supper in the dining hall.

The other phase of kibbutz life that impressed me very much is that members who have any special inclination or talent may study towards a profession with every possible support from the kibbutz. Tzippy of Gevi'im is a graduate of the Bezalel School of Design (an academic institution of higher learning); she works for a group of kibbutzim in planning and designing housing interiors and those of public facilities. Yaela of Mishmar HaEmek is interested in dining hall operation; consequently she participates in seminars and takes courses in food technology and kitchen/dining hall management to enable her to do her very best. Yaela's husband has been on a study mission in the United States to learn more about dairy farming; Tzippy's husband, the economist of the kibbutz, has had university training in the field to prepare him for this vital role. Artists and musicians are given opportunities to study privately in academies in Haifa, Tel Aviv and Jerusalem. There are also kibbutzniks who are able to study in universities and even hold positions related to their various disciplines outside their kibbutzim. And finally, in special situations, members are able to secure leaves of absence for a limited period. I found these case histories in their own setting, as told by my kibbutz friends, fascinating and rather revealing of the kibbutz movement's continued strength in the Israeli social system.

The one kibbutz that, in a very small way, has something of myself in it is the new settlement of Yahel, deep in the Arava. The Reform Jewish movement founded it and nurtures it, and I myself made a small token contribution to help get it started. About a year after its dedication—which I was unable to attend—I welcomed a chance to visit Yahel with its founding father, Rabbi Alan Levine. The forty-five young pioneers, against incredible odds, are making a fact out of a dream. After only one year's work, they had all the basics of life—many of which were lacking at the official beginning—and the rudiments of a multifaceted economy, fortified by plenty of commitment and ambition. They grow onions, peppers, and chrysanthemums for export and tomatoes for domestic consumption. A grove of 440 date palms has been planted; grounds are being landscaped, and amenities for body and soul are one by one being introduced. The clubroom is new; nurse's and doctor's weekly visits are a welcome feature of their developing social organization. A swimming pool is being contemplated; summer temperatures in the Arava can reach 145 degrees Fahrenheit.

The patches of green fields are a testimony to these young Israelis' spirit and guts. I thrilled to the sight of them. I marveled at the ease and efficiency with which they conduct their affairs, the enormous amount of hard work they apply to their tasks. They chose the kibbutz way of life; they chose their own religious orientation. They chose their location in an undisputed area, fifty kilometers north of Eilat and bordering on Jordan; they chose to organize their own enterprise. Yahel's young people are determined to make a success of it. From what I saw on this visit, I can well visualize the fruits of their efforts: an exciting experiment that has become a wholesome expression of a kibbutz way of life.

Our part-time residency in Israel began informally in 1969 when we rented a seashore villa in Herzlia for a year. When we took possession of our own flat in Jerusalem in 1970, we suddenly had one foot firmly planted in the country. Because we had visited many times before we became part-time residents, we do not feel compelled to do any sightseeing merely for its own sake. My excursions within the country are undertaken rather as a personal convenience or with a personal connection. So it was with the kibbutzim.

A visit to Yamit[23] came about because someone at a dinner party expressed curiosity regarding it. Ora Goitein, Kitty Falk and I decided to go, in my car, both to see Yamit and because the scenery on the way would make this trip an attractive one. The Cidors, Ruth and Hanan, whose grandson was Yamit's resident doctor, joined us, making this excursion a two-car caravan over desert terrain, through Bedouin settlements and crossing the Gaza Strip. Under brilliant sunlight, in a vast sea of beige sand and bordered by the true blue Mediterranean, Yamit was sprouting out of the ground before our eyes. At age one, this newest developing townlet had about 150 families and singles (about 750 persons) and was housed and served in about 160 new units. Only about forty kilometers from El Arish in Sinai, Yamit was not yet economically self-sufficient. However, on its superb beach the basic framework for a café, shaded areas and other necessary facilities were in the making; Yamit is scheduled to be a thriving community not only supported by a small industry but catering to tourists and vacationers.

A political happening, this settlement was designed to be the hub of ten others in this area. Now, however, after the Carter-engineered Begin/Sadat breakthrough at Camp David and as a consequence of the Israeli/Egyptian peace treaty of March 1979, major territorial changes are clearly indicated. Yamit's transfer to Egyptian sovereignty is one of several heartbreaking accommodations that must be made in the pursuit of peace.

Another excursion to Sharm el Sheik represented the most travel time I had ever spent anywhere, in one of the least traveled areas in Israel. On an impulse, I decided to visit the tip of Sinai—I had already made a flying visit to Santa Katarina with Harold and some friends—and invited my houseguest and Dorith to accompany me for the weekend. Dorit did most of the driving. We all enjoyed immensely the spectacular scenery, especially from Eilat to Sharm: the Red Sea on one side and the rugged terrain of Sinai in a kaleidoscope of changing colors and shapes on the other. We had a feeling of vast distance and absolute timelessness every kilometer we covered. We stayed in Eilat two nights, en route to and from Sharm. The awesomeness of Sinai, the boat ride, the fabulous underwater sea life, the company of a young soldier (a recent immigrant from Madrid with whom I could converse only in French) and the political significance of Sharm itself all added up to a meaningful experience that I shall long remember.

I would never have seen the inside of a prison had I not had the opportunity to visit a VIP involved in a white-collar scandal that rocked the nation and helped unseat the Labor government. We had met Asher Yadlin at the first Prime Minister's Economic Conference in 1968 and gotten to know him well during the time Harold worked with him in Hevrat Ovdim, the umbrella organization of all economic enterprises of Histadrut.[24] He was one of the ablest of the younger leaders of the country; a bright future was predicted for him. A man of dedication, he derived his ideals and strength from his kibbutz background. Unhappily, Asher got himself into trouble and is currently serving a five-year sentence for fraud and tax evasion.

In the memorable visit with him in Ramle Prison, Harold and I found him in a reflective mood with much inner stability after having performed the hardest part of his ordeal, the admission of his guilt. He was fully aware of the stupidity and the wrong of his action, and of the damage he had brought on himself and his country. He also believed that, having been vulnerable, he was taking the rap for many others high in the political hierarchy. Asher is recharging himself with study (French and math) and with writing his story; he is also an exemplary prisoner, performing a job commensurate with his ability.

We took him chocolates, duty-free cigarettes and freeze-dried instant coffee; prison protocol, however, didn't allow gifts for inmates. Anyway, Asher insisted that he lacked for nothing; he missed nothing at all. Only his freedom. During the hour we were together, he was happy to review with us the many pleasant and fruitful occasions of collaboration in connection with Harold's role as consultant to Hevrat Ovdim (where he was its general manager) on managerial and manufacturing problems. Remembering something of the good in himself made him confident of the future. He is ready, upon his release, to make positive contributions to society, as he had done all his life before his downfall. I was so moved by this confrontation, one of the many of the human condition, that I wished I could do something toward his rehabilitation.

We have had friends in the Tel Aviv area ever since David Uriely was our water drilling business partner in 1954. We are still in touch with his family. A friend of David's, a self-made man of stature and a successful industrialist as well as an art patron, the late Ze'ev Grodecky in the fifties was a frequent visitor in the United States, once even our guest in Pittsburgh. Already in business with David (Near Eastern Drilling Company), Harold was influenced by Grodecky also to invest in America House, then still a dream of his. A partner of Grodecky's in Amcor/Ampa (electrical appliances manufacturing enterprise), Shimon Elman, and his wife, Aviva, with whom we share many interests (art collecting for one), later became personal friends of ours, too. Grodecky's and Elman's daughters and sons-in-law, the Norbert (Zelma) Rubinsteins and Jitzchak (Yael) Moritzes, are also in our small circle of Tel Aviv friends. Through the years, Moritz has become our business lawyer as well.

Even before we invested in Rehovoth Instruments in 1967, we had met the man who later became its scientific director, Dr. Joseph H. Jaffe, world-renowned spectroscopist who was then associated with the Weizmann Institute. The Jaffes (Hali and Joe are both scientists) and we saw much of each other in earlier years; we had through them also a close look at the Weizmann Institute. We still meet occasionally, though Joe and we are no longer in a business relationship.

Ora and Ben Cohen, two of the youths who fought in the 1948 War of Liberation (as did the Jaffees), are also among our younger friends with whom we have many interests in common. Energetic and devoted, Benny was involved in behind-the-scenes operations in New York City in behalf of the soon-to-be Jewish State. He has done graduate work in the States and has worked under Harold's guidance in several of his business enterprises. Benny is an expert in management and administration; Ora is an industrial psychologist. His connection with El Al has on a number of occasions proved to be very helpful to me in cutting through red tape.

The first Prime Minister's Economic Conference (popularly dubbed the "Millionaires' Conference") was convened in Jerusalem by Prime Minister Levi Eshkol in the spring of 1968. Its stated objective was to accelerate investment in Israel and expand its foreign trade. As Harold was vitally concerned with many aspects of the conference, I attended most of the sessions and all of the social events in conjunction with it, meeting people with whom we had had previous connections, including Robert Nathan of Washington, the distinguished international economist.

We also met men important in the world of trade and commerce and finance. I recall well several informal sessions with Lord Sieff (Spencer and Marks) of London, Sigmund Warburg, also of London, and Astore Mayer of Milan. This was during the 1969 Economic Conference which was convened under the aegis of the new Prime Minister, Golda Meir. Since she and we had already been acquainted (through Ze'ev Sharef), our associations at this time extended beyond the strict formalities of the Conference.

Harold continued to be active in Conference councils and Israel's economy. In 1968 and 1969 he spent considerable time in Israel making (1) surveys of the steel and steel-fabricating industries and (2) a thorough study of management in general. At one time, he was consultant to Bedek (Israel Aircraft Industries) and another time to Hevrat Ovdim. This was during a period in his own career when he was between companies: he had sold the United Steel and Wire Company and did not become Chairman, President and Chief Executive Officer of his present company, AVM, until several years later.

In 1969 we rented a large villa with a beautiful exotic garden. It was back to back with Abba Eban's home, across the road from the Sharon Hotel swimming pool, and faced the Mediterranean. Here on the Herzlia seashore Harold lived when he came alone on business, and here we vacationed together, and with all the children during the summer of 1969. We contemplated buying a villa or a flat, thus further extending the idea of having a foothold in Israel. Harold suggested acquiring this Herzlia property; much to his chagrin, I rejected any such idea. My heart was set on living in newly reunited Jerusalem. We consulted family, and Israeli and American friends. We dealt with real estate agents and saw dozens of desirable properties. Finally, we decided upon a large flat on the top floor of a new building overlooking the Old City. Our trials and tribulations[25] with the contractor would have been comic if they hadn't been so frustrating. With hardly a dollar lost—a minor miracle—we eventually withdrew from this transaction and quickly found another flat.

We have known Hanna and Sid Avihai, for many years neighbors across the street, ever since the first economic conference, where Sid was the majordomo, running the show in his capacity as liaison from the Prime Minister's Office. A younger man than we, personable and bright, Canadian-born Sid represents the successful integration of a young, idealistic immigrant. They both started on a kibbutz; later he served his country in several capacities at home and abroad, earning a Ph.D. along the way. Sid has been teaching at Bar Ilan and Hebrew Universities and has also served in a high administrative post at the latter. Currently he is world Chairman of Keren Hayesod,[26] one of the top positions in Israel. In the many hats he has worn in recent years, he has displayed his keen knack for organization that is both efficient and pleasing. Civic and educational campaigns and fund-raising projects all benefit from his enthusiasm and input. From time to time, I have especially appreciated his helpfulness in getting me to the right persons at the right time about projects in which I am involved. Through him I became interested in supporting the Liberty Bell Garden project in Jerusalem.

Katharine Sonneborn Falk is everyone's Pittsburgh connection.

After having been one of Pittsburgh's leading citizens for many years, she left it in 1947 but returned on many occasions as speaker at UJA, Hadassah and Israel Bond functions, and for personal reasons. Through her activities in behalf of Jewish causes on national and international levels, her M.A. earned at Brandeis University and her avid reading, Kitty Falk has become extremely knowledgeable on Jewish and general history and issues affecting the Jewish people.

Kitty's Arab house[27] in Abu Tor quarter was on the Jordanian border until the city's reunification in 1967. Originally built four hundred years ago as a sheik's house, it has gone through many transformations, and Kitty has modernized it without altering its character. From the top of her living room dome there is a breathtaking view of the Old City; the property has become a landmark. Entertaining simply and with warmth, Kitty is a much admired hostess. She is kind, caring and confidence inspiring. I find her directness also attractive. Since we began to spend much time in Jerusalem, she and we have become personal friends, discovering also that we have mutual friends both in Pittsburgh and in Jerusalem. She is vitally interested in every facet of the civic/cultural life of Jerusalem, where she has made her permanent home since 1965.

About the time we moved one foot into Jerusalem, Kitty's daughter, Ellen Hirsch, and her family also settled there. Quite apart from their relationship, I find my friendship with Ellen a comfortable and rewarding one. She is the only one in my Jerusalem circle half way in years between my children and me. Having children of her own, she typifies the trend of thinking that is the bridge for me between the generations. This bridge is sometimes reassuring, sometimes revealing, occasionally even disturbing. In any case, it's reality. Ellen is a creative cook and entertains frequently with finesse and natural charm.

Ellen and Kitty both prove that first impressions of aloofness can be totally misleading. I am content to have discovered behind the cool exterior the real person of warmth and understanding.

I first met Edwin Herbert Samuel, second Viscount of Mt. Carmel and Toxteth, when he addressed the local chapter of

Hadassah in our Pittsburgh penthouse home in 1969. Lord
Samuel, at the time a visiting lecturer at the University of
Pittsburgh Graduate School of Public and International Affairs,
gave a terrific talk and charmed us all with his suave manner,
sharp wit and warm personality. I was delighted finally to meet
him in person, for, during the year he spent in Pittsburgh, I had
done much traveling, and our paths nowhere crossed in the Jewish
Community, even though he was a favorite of hostesses and on
the lecture platform. After the meeting, he and I discussed our
collection of paintings by Israeli artists, and later I picked up the
London Times that he inadvertently left behind—and these two
incidents brought Edwin and Hadassah (the Lady's name) and us
together. *Mr.* Samuel (as he prefers to be called in Jerusalem)
invited himself and his wife to our home the next day for Shabat
dinner, the last night before their departure from Pittsburgh.

Edwin (or Nebi as we later called him) has spent a lifetime
(over sixty-five years) in Jerusalem, including twenty-eight of the
Mandate and all the years since the founding of the State. He has
had a distinguished career as a public servant and as a successful
author.[28] He also maintains the English side of his life: he sits in
the House of Lords, spending the spring of each year in London.
Once when Harold and I were there, Nebi arranged for us to visit
the House of Lords. Not only did I see the Lord Chancellor's
ceremonious entry—knee breeches, three-cornered hat, mace,
seal and all—but I also heard a debate in the Chamber and
lunched with Nebi and Hadassah in the Lords' dining room.
Later, he took us on a personal tour of medieval Westminster
Hall, the largest banquet room in Europe. In Jerusalem, he has
taken me through the Armenian and Jewish quarters of the Old
City, sharing with me, as it were, some of his personal
recollections of life in Old Jerusalem. Spry in body and mind,
Nebi is a talented raconteur; his knowledge and reminiscences are
a rare treat. His wife, Hadassah, was born in Jaffa before Tel Aviv
was founded. She speaks, not only her native Hebrew and
flawless French, but also an impeccable English which she
learned upon becoming a Lady. She is a personality in her own
right and great fun to be with. Only recently, I took her on a two-

day excursion to Rosh Pina and Kibbutz Mishmar HaEmek, where we visited with Edwin's niece. We also got to know Hadassah's niece Ruth Horam, an accomplished younger artist, and her husband, suave and charming Foreign Office official Yehuda (ex-Ambassador to Korea and Greece).

The Samuels, both near eighty, are gracious hosts; their Shabat afternoon tea parties are delightful occasions for spirited conversation and for meeting interesting people. This is how, many years ago, we became acquainted with Mr. Joie de Vivre himself, Ze'ev Vilnay, the popular geographer and historian, and his lovely wife, Esther. The Samuels are responsible for my having met two members of the Rothschild dynasty under the most pleasant circumstances: Baron Edmond, who comes to Jerusalem frequently on museum business, and Baroness Alix, who lives in the Yemin Moshe quarter. Never a dull moment with Edwin and Hadassah.*

In one of the strangest coincidences of my life, I met a friend from more than thirty years ago at the Centennial Observance (1976) of the Hebrew Union College in Jerusalem: Carl Hermann Voss. Born and raised in Pittsburgh, Carl is a Protestant minister, a college professor and author of eight books and innumerable articles; at that time he was a resident scholar on behalf of the National Conference of Christians and Jews at the Ecumenical Institute for Advanced Theological Studies at Tantur, on the southern edge of Jerusalem on the way to Bethlehem. Carl, Harold and I, though not classmates (he being four years ahead of us), had mutual friends among the Pitt faculty and shared the same convictions in the 1930s as well as in subsequent years when our paths diverged. Active in many causes of common interest, he became committed to one cause, however, which I didn't then espouse, Zionism.

Carl left his Pittsburgh pastorate in 1943 to work in church-related programs in the field of peace and international friendship. He has always been a dedicated Christian friend of Israel and for more than 35 years has been closely identified with all the

*As the typescript of this book was being readied for the printer, we received a telephone call from London informing us of Edwin Samuel's death in Jerusalem the week before.

prominent personalities of the movement. An ecumenical leader and a dynamic speaker, he has devoted himself to the fate and the future of the Jewish people. At present, in work at Tantur, at the Hebrew University (of which he is an Honorary Fellow!) and at the Centre for Postgraduate Hebrew Studies at Oxford, England, he has been completing research for his forthcoming book on American Christians for and against Zionism. As he and his wife, Phyllis, live in Florida, we most often have our reunions in Jerusalem, where we enjoy some of the same personal relationships. We count Phyllis and Carl among our dearest friends.

We have long been friends with Hanan and Ruth Cidor. Originally Berliners, they spent many years in Israel's Foreign Service, he at one time having been ambassador at The Hague. There is an old-world charm about this couple, an old-fashioned gentility that I find appealing. She had been a student of the Bauhaus in her youth; they are as up-to-date as tomorrow in their interest in art. We served together with Hanan—and with the Samuels and Kitty Falk—on the Israeli committee for the creation of the Israel Room at the University of Pittsburgh. When the Cidors came to Pittsburgh to confer on the plans, we had the pleasure of entertaining for them. Since then, due to budget problems, the project has been laid aside for the time being. What the Cidors probably remember most, however, is the helicopter ride over the city and out to Nemacolin Inn for lunch with Al and Connie Rockwell. Hanan was the Israeli government's liaison in the establishment of the Ecumenical Institute for Advanced Theological Studies at Tantur in Jerusalem. He saw it to completion and launched its academic program.

We knew Rose Sheshkin in New York City back in the sixties, when she had an art gallery in the Upper East Seventies. Rose and her husband, Miron, emigrated to Israel in 1969 and settled in Jerusalem, where his varied career in political Zionist activities for over forty years automatically opened many important doors for them. The Dr. Sheshkins are old-time political associates of Prime Minister Menachem Begin. His work with the Jewish Agency, his writings, and Rose's art involvements make them creative contributors to the political, artistic and social life of the capital. Heartily hospitable, they attract all sorts of interesting people; their evenings "at home," especially on Fridays, are happy times.

Another hub of delightful encounters is the distinctive home of the Dr. Rafaelis. Whether it's strictly social or a benefit for young Israeli musicians, Esther's and Alex's hospitality is synonymous with warmth and style. She is Australian born and he is originally from Riga; he arrived in the thirties and served in the U.S. Army while an Israeli student in America. They, like many of our Jerusalem friends, are widely traveled, speak several languages well and know many of the same people. This is precisely why I find my life in Jerusalem such an exciting maze of human relationships.

We met the De Vrieses in their home city of Amsterdam on our first trip abroad and have gotten to know them well through frequent reunions in Europe, Pittsburgh and Jerusalem, where they settled in 1966. Concentration camp survivors, they achieved much success in their personal lives and left a comfortable life in Holland for Israel out of conviction, not economic need. A lawyer by profession, Izsak travels abroad annually in behalf of the Jewish Agency, in connection with his private law practice or just to visit family. Their fluency in five languages is phenomenal; they, with the Cidors and Rafaelis, are the most cosmopolitan people I know anywhere. It was Izsak and Fré, two wonderful human beings, who urged us to follow their example and establish ourselves in Jerusalem. Over the years, they have been most kind in introducing us to a wide circle of their friends; until her death recently, Fré was an incomparable hostess in the classic tradition and a tireless worker for the Lifeline for the Old.

Among the people whom we got to know well through the De Vrieses are Burt and Rabbi Israel Goldstein, who themselves are the nucleus of a remarkable social circle. A long-time pillar of the Conservative Jewish movement in the United States, Israel is an author, one of the founders of Brandeis University and active in political Zionist circles. He left his pulpit in New York to settle permanently in Jerusalem about eighteen years ago. Our personal connection with them has been a most pleasant one.

The temptation to refer to rabbis in a group is irresistible. And so to complete the list of our most active social groups in Jerusalem, I cite Bella and Richard G. Hirsch and Shirley and Ezra Spicehandler. Our friendship with them originally rose from our interest in the Reform Jewish movement. We first met the Hirsches in Washington through mutual friends who believed we simply had to know them; they were right. Author and public person, Dick was the speaker (What dynamism!) at Eddie's ordination service. When they emigrated in 1972, we were already settled in our miniflat. Dick, Executive Director of the World Union for Progressive Judaism, is a forceful spokesman for non-Orthodoxy in Israel and active in Israeli politics. Ezra, just a little less young than Dick, is an amateur archaeologist, author and eminent academic. Also the only person I know whose name is mentioned in the book *O Jerusalem,*[29] Ezra is Dean of the Jerusalem School of the Hebrew Union College. He and I share a very personal dilemma: weight control.

We are fortunate to have found ourselves in the personally rewarding company of the many dear friends we have in Jerusalem and elsewhere in Israel, including those not here mentioned!

Chapter 15

Art Collecting

It is difficult to pinpoint when and how our art collecting began. It was not a moment in time but rather a condition that grew and evolved over a number of years, taking shape and substance as we ourselves developed in our tastes and grew in knowledge. Harold and I both have been exposed to art from our youth. I remember well my visiting the early Carnegie Internationals in Pittsburgh in the thirties and forties and browsing around in the Metropolitan Museum of Art on my occasional trips to New York City. I began to enjoy museum hopping when we were young marrieds and had reason to be in Washington on union business. When we lived there during World War II, we frequently visited the (Mellon) National Gallery of Art, which was then still relatively new. I expanded my experience further when our travels included Boston and Chicago as well. The Impressionists and Postimpressionists attracted me most, as very little of those schools was included in the art appreciation course I took at Pitt. On one of those exceedingly torrid and humid days in Washington, reluctant to leave the relative cool and serenity of the National Gallery, I am supposed to have asked, "Why don't we set up housekeeping here?'' Wouldn't it be nice to live in an art gallery?'' we asked each other. Today, we do. In both of our homes.

We had received from my parents several nineteenth-century

and turn-of-the-century paintings of the academic tradition. In spite of our tight budget, we later bought from a distant relative in Chicago a large oil painting, *The Slave Market* by Mozart Rottman—our first acquisition. We had no concept yet of the genre of art that we preferred, nor any idea of how we would finance an art-collecting venture. Foreign travel and a somewhat more generous budget in the late fifties, though, helped to give our vague ideas practical expression. Thus, in the old quarter of Stockholm we bought a striking cityscape, *The Square in Front of the Opera* by Jansen. We were no longer buying reproductions of famous paintings *(The Night Watchman, The Jewish Bride, Maja Naked, Maja Clothed,* Van Gogh's *Chair and Drawbridge)* and relegated what we had to the children's rooms. At this time, too, we were buying quality souvenirs of our foreign tours, such as silver, vicuna fur, ivory, small antiques, precious jewelry and watches. We had not yet, in the early sixties, decided what we really wanted to collect. We knew only that we came on the scene too late for the Impressionists and Postimpressionists. Neither were we at ease with the contemporary schools of Abstract and Op Art.

We had made many trips to Europe, had visited South America and had been around the world once when in 1964 I became cochairman of the Israeli art exhibition sponsored by Temple Sinai in Pittsburgh. A reputable art dealer from Jerusalem in partnership with a young gallery owner in Boston provided the art and the know-how. My cochairman, a large committee, and I executed the ambitious project, bringing an art event to the community and at the same time making a handsome profit for Sinai—both worthy goals. I didn't know then that I would later meet some of the artists whose work I promoted on this occasion. The whole experience, including the purchase of several paintings, became for me an introduction to the art of Israel.

The more we got involved with Israel and the more knowledgeable we grew, the more attractive the idea of seriously collecting art of Israel became. For advice at this early stage, we turned to Yona Mach, a well-known Jerusalem artist and teacher who was also a friend of Daphna's. Through his enthusiasm and knowledge, we gained an invaluable orientation to the history, trends and personalities of the Israeli art scene. This exposure was also the start of a friendship between Esther and Yona and us.

We no longer had any reproductions hanging anywhere in our home; we now were more interested in art books and books on art. By the mid-sixties, we were ready to narrow acquisitions down to a specific category, namely, works by artists identified with Israel: oils, watercolors, lithographs and silkscreens, etchings and drawings. Occasionally, however, we bought something that had an irresistible pull for us even if it didn't fit into our specific area of interest. Ours is therefore a collection principally of art of Israel. The exceptions to the rule are a rather significant lot, including a dozen Picasso plates and jugs (bought in Vallauris at the Madura shop); original signed prints by Picasso, Pissaro, Pascin, Chagall, Gross, the Soyer brothers, Shahn, Serrano and Giacometti; and oils, watercolors and etchings by Jewish artists of the École de Paris—Mintschine, Milich, Mishonce—and by Gross, Shahn and the Soyer brothers.

We were in and out of galleries in Paris, London, Tel Aviv, Jerusalem, on Fifty-seventh Street and Madison Avenue in New York City. We were exploring and studying contemporary art, very often other than Israeli. We were also reading the catalogues and reviews of exhibitions and other events that we couldn't attend in person. By the late sixties, art for us had become a passionate hobby. By then, too, we had some capital to draw on, and we could indulge in the luxury of making purchases whenever the opportunity presented itself. We were beginning to be known by artists, galleries and museum people as collectors; eventually, we accepted ourselves as collectors.

All through the years, we made every effort to upgrade the quality of our collection, seeking always the best available examples of an artist's work and, if possible, including many periods of it. At the same time, we rejected any piece that we couldn't both live with; our own sense of aesthetics had to be satisfied before any other consideration. Sometimes in the selection process, Harold and I didn't agree at first on a major purchase; after much deliberation we would "compromise" by either buying it or rejecting it. It also happened now and then that afterwards one of us regretted our decision. But, as we intended always for this collection to be a mutual undertaking, we learned to live with our decisions and to enjoy the results.

In the upgrading process, some paintings were traded back to the gallery or the artist himself in exchange for works we wanted even more. Shortly after the 1970 Carnegie International, we completed the upgrading, and the character of our collection was pretty well set. We had chosen the Israeli artists whose works we were collecting in depth. We had also acquired a couple of dozen sculptures by Agam, Gross, Trobe, Orloff and Gruber.

Renee and Chaim Gross, our non-Israeli artist friends, live in a converted warehouse on the edge of Greenwich Village (New York City), the ground floor of which is his studio and workshop (but not foundry). It is also a large exhibition room containing hundreds of his sculptures and providing storage for watercolors, sketches and lithographs he has done in the past. The objects in wood (most of them in exotic species such as paloblanco and sabicu ebony) are unique pieces; the bronzes are duplicates of original castings. On the two upper floors is the residence, abundantly furnished and notable for an outstanding collection of paintings by other prominent artists, including several friends of the Grosses, and by their son-in-law Red Grooms. His large collection of African figurines, parts of which are often out on loan to museums, is attractively displayed in glass-fronted cases along walls and in niches.

The Grosses are two dear people who envelope you with their concern and affection for you. We find many subjects of mutual interest, and, when we are together, in conversation or on an excursion, time seems to fly by fast. Chaim's reputation as a dintinguished American artist and our close connection led to our commissioning him to create a seven-foot-high Menorah for Temple Sinai. It is a graceful but striking representation of a traditional nine-branched candelabrum. Two of the original castings are placed in the sanctuary and one rises outside the building. The Menorah has become Temple Sinai's logo. A two-foot-high maquette of the Sinai Menorah, also in bronze, stands on a Jerusalem rock—chiseled by Harold—in our miniflat as a silent but bright reminder of our Pittsburgh life. Another casting of this Menorah, the sculptor's own, was shown in the Gross Retrospective Exhibition in the New York Jewish Museum during the 1976–77 season, as an example of his synagogue art. From our private collection, Gross picked for this exhibition a small sculpture, *Homage to Chagall.*

In addition to the artists we get to know, another fringe benefit of art collecting is the recognition we receive. Gifts we have made—Gross's Menorahs to Temple Sinai being the first—bring us as much enjoyment as the recipient (and the public) derives from them. *Self-Portrait* by Ardon, donated to the Israel Museum, has been shown in exhibition twice. Agam's *Life Is a Passing Shadow* is on permanent view at the Scaife Gallery of Carnegie Museum in Pittsburgh.

A series of Gross hand-colored lithographs hangs in halls of the Hebrew Union College in Jerusalem; a series on the Jewish Holidays, also hand-colored lithographs by Gross, is prominently displayed at Temple Sinai. There, too, hangs a striking basalt and oil bas-relief painting done by Moshe Castel in 1960; it represents a view of the Dead Sea looking up towards Jerusalem. It was formally dedicated at a Friday evening service. Gruber's Plexiglas kinetic sculpture is shown in the Rose Museum of Fine Arts at Brandeis University. Sempere's kinetic composition is placed in the courtyard of a community center in Jerusalem. And a golden Menorah shines in the President's House in Jerusalem; I shall tell the story behind it separately.

Loans from our collection, another means of sharing our art with the public, began with the Venice Biennale in 1968: *Sunset* by Ardon. We are pleased to be asked for loans and spare no expense in carrying out requests for them. If possible, we attend the exhibition, setting up our travel plans accordingly. Thus, we went to see the *Sunset* in Venice but were unable to follow the *Shadow* as it passed from city to city to the end of its trail, Tel Aviv. The *Shadow*'s beginning was in Harold's mind on one Yom Kippur afternoon when, between formal services, readings from the prayer book occupied our attention. A passage from *Midrash:*

Genesis Rabbah 80 Harold found especially meaningful, and he decided that it might be an appropriate theme for artistic expression. It goes like this: "Life Is A Passing Shadow: The Shadow of a tower or a tree? No: the shadow of a bird—for when a bird flies away, there is neither shadow nor bird."

We consequently commissioned Agam to create a painting or a sculpture on this theme in 1967; he was still working on it when Leon Arkus, Director of the Carnegie Museum of Art, went abroad on his "shopping" tour for the 1970 Carnegie International. Leon picked our double-sided kinetic *Shadow* (72 by 115 centimeters, set at eye level on a pedestal) in its half-completed state, not knowing for whom or where it was intended. Neither could he guess that eventually it would find its permanent home in the Carnegie Museum. Between the time that he spotted the *Shadow* in Agam's atelier and its arrival in Pittsburgh, we passsed through Paris twice in order to keep Agam working on it. By now he had such a worldwide reputation that he could hardly keep up with the many commissions he had accepted.

We couldn't risk Agam's neglecting our *Shadow* in favor of a monumental piece designed for Munich or Sao Paulo. Entertaining him at the popular and chic Crazy Horse Saloon nightclub was one way to keep his mind and hands on our art. On an another occasion, in a restaurant, he drew a portrait of me on a napkin, which he offered to pay for (he didn't have to). He unfortunately endowed me with an unflattering extra chin; for this reason, vain and foolish as this may seem, this precious work of art never sees the light of day.

Before 1978 came to a close, Harold and I agreed to de-acquisition several more important pieces from our collection. An oversized abstract, titled *In the Beginning,* by Samuel Rosenberg; a small oil painting from his Rouault period, titled *My Brother's Keeper,* and several lithographs by Zvi Milstein and Anatole Kaplan were given to Temple Sinai. The Israel Museum in Jerusalem gladly accepted an assortment of Jakob Steinhardt oils, drawings and etchings from his Berlin period. And finally, Carnegie Museum in Pittsburgh was pleased to accept a large oil, *Intimate Concert,* by Moses Soyer and several lithographs including a Chagall, a Giacometti and a Dali.

After the 1970 International was over, we were asked by the French National Museum of Modern Art to lend the *Shadow* (featured on the preview invitations) for a tour of Paris, Amsterdam, Düsseldorf and Tel Aviv, where we viewed it with much pleasure. After an absence of nine months, *Shadow* returned to our penthouse, becoming the most traveled piece of art in our entire collection. It moved with us to Fifth Avenue, but soon after that we made a gift of it to the Carnegie Museum on occasion of the opening of its Scaife Wing in October, 1975. Here, no longer our property, appropriately displayed, it is even more popular than it was during its loan days. The feedback we get from individual museum visitors, docents and guards is tremendously gratifying. Our pleasure in the gift is as great as that which was ours in its ownership. We also enjoy making gifts of art from our collection to our children.

Other exhibitions, besides the Venice Biennale and the Carnegie International, in which we participated are:

- Fima *Self-Portrait* in "Self-Portraits" exhibit, 1972, Haifa Museum
- Three Fima compositions in his one-man show, 1972, Israel Museum, Jerusalem
- Four oils on canvas, examples of calligraphy compositions, in Fima one-man show, 1972, Jewish Museum, New York City
- *The Passing Shadow* by Agam; *The Empty Room* and *There Is No Prophet In his Town* by Bergner, *The Arab Fisherman*[30] by Rubin in "The Jewish Experience of the Twentieth Century" exhibit, 1975–76, Jewish Museum, New York City
- Six paintings by Castel chosen from both our Pittsburgh and our Jerusalem collections, in his retrospective scheduled for October, 1973,[31] but held in March, 1974, Tel Aviv Museum
- Two Agam sculptures in "Sculpture We Live with" exhibition (works privately owned in the Pittsburgh area), 1968, Carnegie Museum, Pittsburgh
- Drawings by Pascin and Walkowitz, in "Art in Resi-

dence" exhibit (works privately owned in the Pittsburgh area), 1963, Carnegie Museum, Pittsburgh

- Four large oils by Castel, S. Rosenberg, M. Soyer, and Fima, in "Pittsburgh Corporations Collect" exhibit, 1975, Carnegie Museum, Pittsburgh
- Kinetic sculpture by Sempere, in inaugural exhibit of Tel Aviv Museum, 1972
- *Homage to Chagall* by Gross (small sculpture), Gross Retrospective exhibit, 1977, Jewish Museum, New York City
- *To the Morning Star* and *Sunset* by Ardon (On the road again!), Ardon Retrospective exhibit, 1978, Staatliche Kunsthalle, Berlin, West Germany.

During 1970 and 1971, when Israel's presidential residence (Beit Hanassi) was being constructed, we used to visit our artist friends at their studios and on location when they were at work on their own contributions to the house. We were quite familiar with three major works of art in the reception hall even before the house was formally inaugurated: Castel's two basalt bas-relief murals at opposite ends (one in cool grey blue and one in warm gold), Bezem's sixty-three panels in the ceiling, and Rubin's vitrage. Three years later, we were personally involved with art in Beit Hanassi when President Ephraim Katzir accepted our donation of a piece of sculpture by Agam.

By then, Agam's work in the Élysée Palace (official residence of the President of France) had been well publicized. We commissioned him to make us a medium-sized Menorah to be placed within Beit Hanassi; his *Hundred Gates,* also a donation, already stood in the garden. We were pleased to know that our offer was acceptable and looked forward to the presentation ceremony in May, 1976.

The President walked into the reception hall at the appointed hour and, after conversing with us, mingled with the assembled guests. A prominent scientist on leave from the Weizmann Institute, a handsome man and a natural host, he put everyone at ease with his unaffected, friendly manner—as if he were having us in his own home for a private party. President Katzir has a knack for remembering people: later, at Sharef's birthday party, a friend offered to introduce me to him when he suddenly extended his hand to me in a friendly greeting and spoke animatedly of the golden Menorah being a big hit since its presentation.

In a moment of hushed anticipation, the Menorah was unveiled; it was then wheeled back into the adjacent smaller reception room. Fruit juices, soft drinks, cognac and cookies were served; we sat down, and the twenty minutes alloted to us stretched to an hour's visit. To our astonishment, Professor Katzir, flanked on either side by Harold and myself, not only made some appreciative remarks but asked us to speak about ourselves for a few minutes. We have no record of this presidential chitchat or of our remarks, but the total experience for us, as well as for our guests, was one we all remember with much pleasure. The Menorah, a gold-plated sculpture whose eighteen movable branches have a maximum spread of 130 centimeters, stands on a pedestal in the large reception hall. It is, I am told, greatly admired by all who are honored and entertained by the President of Israel in his House. A gold-plated maquette of it, 19½ centimeters high with a maximum spread of 25 centimeters, is displayed in our Pittsburgh home.

Personal contacts between artists and ourselves give us a deeper understanding of the man or woman behind—actually in front of—the canvas. The friendships that have developed are a delightful by-product of our interest in their art.

In Paris, we have sat in the Café Cupole many times with Agam, Gross, Orloff, or Fima and their circle of friends, observing them at their leisure: eating heartily and talking uninhibitedly. Here too, we have visited Agam and Orloff in their spacious ateliers; drunk schnapps with Ardon in his; and dined with Agam and Fima in their homes. We have been guests of Esther and Reuven Rubin in their Tel Aviv home (now a museum) and their huge Caesarea villa; of Bilha and Moshe Castel in their grand Tel Aviv house, which is also his studio, and in New York. The Castels and Horams have also been our weekend guests in Pittsburgh, as has Fima.

In 1969, Reuven Rubin, some other friends and we were lunching in an East Jerusalem restaurant when Mark Chagall and his entourage, including Teddy Kollek, Mayor of Jerusalem, entered. Moments later, Kolleck and Rubin were table hopping, and, as Rubin was a friend of Chagall's, we suddenly found ourselves being introduced to the great master. Almost as exciting was the fact that I was able to converse with him briefly in French. Chagall was also kind enough, a few months later, to sign a *Blue Bird* poster (bought in Monte Carlo) for us through Gross's intercession.

Each time we are in Israel, we meet at least one of our artist friends. We have thus shared in happy family celebrations of Agam and Fima for their sons' Bar Mitzvahs; and have sat with Hanna and Naftali Bezem after the tragic death of their paratrooper son, who was a victim of a terrorist attack in downtown Jerusalem's Zion Square.

Since I got to know Fima's Finnish wife, Kaarina, in Paris and Jerusalem, we see them now and then in both places. We also keep in touch with Ticho and Mach; our paths cross frequently with the Horams, Stateside, the Grosses are friends in a category all its own. With some of our artists, thus, we have maintained a personal relationship far beyond the art that brought us together in the first place. Such social encounters add still another dimension to our daily lives.

We also number among our friends in the art world one couple who are not artists themselves: Miriam and Herbert Goldman of the Goldman Gallery in Haifa. Respected among artists and collectors and in international art circles, the Goldmans are successful dealers, knowledgeable on many levels besides art, peppery, sociable and delightful company. We occasionally meet in Jerusalem; we are their guests when we visit in Haifa; we have hosted them in Pittsburgh. Once recently, Miriam alone visited many cities in the States promoting the sale of Goldman Gallery art especially selected for this tour. We arranged an exhibition/ sale in Pittsburgh at the Michael Berger Gallery, and we had several social affairs promoting her. Art partronage takes many curious forms on the grass-roots level.

The most complex art undertaking on our part was the art auction we held in 1976 for benefit of Temple Sinai. We initiated it, organized it and carried it out with great success. Along the way, we had the enthusiasm of, and countless (wo)man-hours of work by, an able committee assisting us. Being general chairman of the event, I was deeply involved, from selection of pieces of art, through publicity and setup, to the evening of the sale itself. We made available nearly 100 original works of art—mostly lithographs—from our own collection, and Harold himself performed as auctioneer with great aplomb and effectiveness. The art was of exceptionally high quality, and so was the audience. No ordinary commercial art auction, this event was unique, and those who attended supported it to the tune of nearly $10,000 in an atmosphere of serious fun.

Most art collectors commission portraits of themselves and undoubtedly have interesting stories to tell of how their artists were selected. The portraits of Harold and of myself, however, were more a case of "just happening" and less a premeditated project. The first family portrait in our collection is actually of my father, done for a large family celebration of his eighty-eighth birthday. This was held in Jerusalem, where both he and we were comfortably settled in our then home away from home, the King David Hotel. Mach, wishing to share in the celebration, painted a forceful likeness of Father—a beautiful study of old age and tranquility.

In less than a year's time, Bezem was our houseguest in Pittsburgh for the dedication of his stained glass window in Temple Sinai. He literally dashed off a portrait of Harold one early morning when the sun shone brightly. His easel was makeshift; his colors and tools had been bought the day before. Harold is caught in one of his whimsical moods, and the painting, on a clear, bight yellow background with bold strokes of black, portrays him, in spite of the lighter vein, as a strong man of action.

While Fima was despondent over his young wife's death, he alternated between hard work and short fits of depression. For a change of mood, he was delighted to do a portrait of Harold and one of me in 1967. We spent several sessions in his sixth-floor atelier/home (no lift) in the Rothschild-funded artist's residence complex on Rue de Barque. He worked furiously, completing the pieces from photographs after we had left Paris. He painted a total of two portraits of Harold and five of me, calling all but one of mine merely "sketches." I think he captured the essence of me in all of the lot. My favorite hangs in our Jerusalem home; the one he likes best he kept for himself.

A round-shaped double portrait of Harold and myself was executed in Jerusalem by Mirian Bat-Yosef. She painted it on stretched silk moiré, giving us a broad background of the scene from our flat: the Valley of the Cross. She showed, not only the Israel Museum and the Knesset, but two Monasteries of the Cross, as if we needed both "hers" and "his" in Pittsburgh to evoke in us our magnificent Jerusalem view. Not only are we both represented on the canvas, but there are two pairs of us, which show us from different angles. When Bat-Yosef was our houseguest in Pittsburgh on her way to Japan, she was kind enough to touch up the scowl on one of my faces, making me appear as relaxed as I more normally am.

Mach painted a portrait of me also with the front view from our Jerusalem flat as background. It captures me in a moment of contemplation on a canvas of clear bright colors and much light. I have not selected a painting of myself as the definitive portrait; perhaps it has not yet been painted. In the meantime, different as they are, all the works speak to me without reserve or embarrassment.

A two-week holiday in the south of France during the late summer of 1969 was for both Harold and me a totally art-oriented one. We enjoyed a pleasant balance of ideal climate, leisurely pursued distractions, and picturesque locale, but art adventures were what made the trip memorable. We constantly had the feeling of close communion with the many works of art of Chagall (who lives in this neighborhood), Leger, Braque, Picasso, Matisse, Calder, Kandinsky and others on exhibition in museums of the region.

Colombe D'Or in St. Paul de Vence is where we stayed; a seventy-mile stretch along the Mediterranean from Menton to St. Tropez and the hill and valley villages behind were the scene of our explorations. This area is now known as having the greatest concentration of modern art per square foot in the world. We had the bridal suite of the inn, fronting on the swimming pool, which had a Braque tilework underwater and a giant Calder mobile on its edge. Hallways, nooks and corners, but especially guests' lounges, dining room and garden were decorated with notable works of art. Some were charming pieces by less celebrated artists, but it is the genius of famous postimpressionists that is the focus of this truly unique holiday resort.

Almost daily we made excursions to places of art interest. Among these were the Leger Museum in Biot, the House of Renoir in Cagnes, the Matisse Chapel in Vence, the Maeght Foundation Museum just outside the village of St. Paul de Vence, and the church in Villefranche-sur-Mer, made famous by Jean Cocteau's total decoration of it. We also spent an unforgettable day in Vallauris, where Picasso used the four walls of an ancient Romanesque chapel as the "canvas" for his 1959 symbolic frescoes called *War and Peace*. Here, too, is Madura, the pottery workshop–studio–market that sells Picasso-created shapes and designs in ceramic. In Vallauris we engaged in a lively argument over the purchase of twelve plates, two jugs and other assorted Picasso works—all signed and numbered, of course. Soon afterwards, I conceded that Harold was right in making this substantial acquisition.

A remarkable art confrontation occurred to Harold and me recently in the least likely place and at the least expected time. Not having had a proper celebration of our fortieth wedding anniversary, we decided to do something for ourselves that we have never done before. In January, 1977, we treated each other to a Caribbean cruise on the S.S. *Doric*. We invited two couples with whom we have been friends for many years to see us off, having made arrangements in advance for a champagne party for the six of us. Persistent rain at the dock in Fort Lauderdale in no way dampened our spirits. Presence of friends, in fact, elevated them considerably. Then, when we embarked, an even greater excitement awaited us. On our way to our cabin, we were astounded to come face to face with a monumental Agam mural in the stairwell, extending over three floors. In one single stroke of recall, we realized that the boat we were about to sail on was the former S.S. *Shalom,* once the proud flagship of Israel. Works of art by L. Schatz and Jean David confirmed our assumption. This was further corroborated later by testimony of the ship's captain. The magnificent staircase mural and the other decorative details were our constant companions on a cruise that introduced us to some Caribbean islands and offered us a much needed total holiday.

Chapter 16

One Foot in Jerusalem

How is it, I sometimes wonder, that no one ever asks me in Jerusalem how we live in Pittsburgh; yet in Pittsburgh we are often quizzed about our activities in Jerusalem. Our two-home existence has created much curiosity among friends and acquaintances; hardly a conversation passes that someone doesn't bring up the subject. Ours is a variation of the commoner practice of maintaining homes in Pittsburgh and Florida. What is it like to live in Jerusalem? What do you do there? And nearly always, the questioner adds, You sure have the best of both worlds!

Harold and I both think we are pretty fortunate. We are able to set our own timing; business demands and family needs as well as our own whims more or less guide our comings and goings. During the past several years, we have been in Jerusalem twice a year, in the spring and in the fall around the High Holydays. Both times, Harold is absent from his office for about three weeks; usually I go ahead of him and stay several weeks after he leaves. Sometimes I return to the States via Europe, where I may meet him or pursue a brief personal mission of my own. After we first set up our Jerusalem household in 1970, we spent two consecutive fall and winter seasons there. During these periods, I enrolled in an Ulpan (an intensive Hebrew language course) but found that, at my age, there was no appreciable improvement.

Since I do not need the language to make a living, to do my shopping or even to get around socially, I decided to study less and enjoy more.

Occasionally, I have a houseguest. Most often, of course, Harold and I, as in our Pittsburgh home, are alone in our miniflat; we enjoy doing what we like and when, without the usual office pressures and community commitments. We combine a brisk social life with the cultural events in which we are interested. There may be someone on a sabbatical from his university or his congregation, or sent by his publisher or research organization; or someone attending an international congress. Or the municipality may have a VIP guest at Mishkenot whom we already know or, if we don't, we may have the opportunity to meet him/her through friends. Interesting people constantly touch our lives.

Some of our friends are collectors of art, antiques, Judaica, archaeology, rare books, ancient maps; some of the same persons are habitual concertgoers and previewers. Our friends are, as in Pittsburgh, well read, articulate and concerned. In Jerusalem we seem to live with the overwhelming sensation of being at the crossroads of political and intellectual stirrings that affect our welfare and destiny. Our life has never been routine. In Pittsburgh, for the most part, it is stimulating. In Jerusalem, for the most part, it is supercharged.

The 504 Peugeot gives us a precious commodity: mobility. We can pick up and go anytime, anywhere. An expensive convenience for one who is only a part-time resident, but the extraordinary benefits I derive from it make it well worth the cost. Driving in Israel, whether in town or on the highways, is at times both dangerous and aggravating, as Israeli driving habits are anything but courteous. Short tempers and abrasiveness are in fact as irritating behind the wheel as they are over the counter or on the telephone. I seem to be rather frequently involved in unpleasant encounters with clerks and secretaries, especially those who are supposed to help the client or the customer but don't. In self-defense, I talk back to rude drivers and other offenders of bad manners without caring whether they understand me or not.

When I was a witness to the Sadat spectacle in Jerusalem, I could not help but remember in great detail the circumstances surrounding my presence there during the Yom Kippur War. Experiencing that conflict at close range four years earlier was a strange prelude to this phenomenal twist of events. For me a curious coincidence, too, that I happened to have been on the scene both times.

Harold and I spent the High Holydays of 1973 in Jerusalem. We were nostalgic for Father—no longer able to make the trip with us, and for the children, who wouldn't have visited with us at this time anyway. All the more did we anticipate this particular time of the year in the midst of family and close friends, in an ambience totally consonant with observance. In 1973, however, there was something completely foreign added to this special season of the year: a full-scale war—a surprise attack—launched by Israel's Arab neighbors on Yom Kippur, the holiest day in the Hebrew calendar.

As our apartment is a bit far for walking to and from the miniflat and Hebrew Union College services during the twenty-five-hour span between nightfall and the last blow of the *shofar,* we spent the night at the YMCA. All private cars and buses return home hours before Yom Kippur to render Jerusalem virtually free of moving vehicles on that day. When in the early morning we heard two low-flying Phantoms zoom past overhead, we were somewhat shaken; we were wondering, but not alarmed.

At the conclusion of the morning service I returned to the YMCA, only a block away, for a brief rest. Upon hearing the wail of the sirens at two different times, I left the YMCA to join in the spirit of the Holyday at the King David Hotel. As I was checking out, I realized that the guests and tourists at the YMCA, all Christians and/or Arabs, had already been hearing war reports since 2:00 P.M. They were stunned and kept mumbling, "The Egyptians and Syrians attacked us."

After spending a few hours listening to the radio communiques and breaking the fast (early) in the company of friends, and calling on other friends on the way, we arrived home in near darkness. I quickly prepared a weekender and a shopping bag with necessities and some indispensable conveniences should we need to go to our shelter. We did, twice, during the next eight days.

Harold stayed by my side until the Israeli Army crossed into Egypt and the Syrians were beaten back on the Golan. We also decided that I would stay until we knew better just how serious the situation was. In the face of hardship and danger I was not inclined to leave friends and family behind.

I was still in Israel when Isaac Stern arrived and made his moving remarks over TV explaining why he couldn't stay away. That afternoon I attended his benefit concert; all public functions took place before dark as strict blackout practices were in effect. Family and friends were all involved in either the army or in support services to aid the war effort. Volunteering was the key to maintaining one's self-respect; everyone was engaged in doing something essential (postal delivery, etc.). I surveyed my possibilities and participated in some of them. But finally, at my family's urging and because I felt an obligation to my aging, sickly father, I became a reluctant El Al passenger eight days after the war began.

It took me just one day in the States to realize that my place was back in Jerusalem. For it was clear to me when I came through customs at Kennedy Airport that calm confidence (the prevailing mood on the wake of the initial shock) was giving way to gloom. This impression became even more pronounced when later I spoke at fund-raising functions and when I discussed the matter with friends at home. Perhaps it was the distance that lent a negative aspect, or perhaps it was the frustration that some of us feel when we can give only money.

In any case, having been satisfied that Harold and Father would be well looked after, and having put all my own personal affairs in order, I made plans to return to Jerusalem without delay. On October 25, the day that President Nixon declared a global alert of all American forces everywhere, accompanied by a friend, Marcia Ripp, I flew out of JFK Airport. I found all of Israel one big family and a wounded soldier or a dead hero or a missing

POW in everyone's immediate circle. The losses, borne with quiet resoluteness, were already staggering. Frustration and anger permeated the atmosphere.

The day after arrival, we began our assault on our objective: to be usefully engaged in the war effort on the civilian front. We succeeded: as soon as my Peugeot 504 was certified as a volunteer vehicle in the national service, we assigned ourselves to the task of driving soldiers on leave to and from their bases. There were two principal dispatch points in Jerusalem and two outside the city from which the soldiers went off to their bases or the front and where they came to be picked up. They traveled two main routes: the Jericho Road and the highway between Jerusalem and Bethel, just past Ramallah. The Jericho Road was the more traveled and was in fact the one we preferred. I learned every bend of this road; I found the climatic changes on it, as well as the shapes and shadings of the desert landscape, a new and stimulating experience each of the over fifty times I drove it.

We chauffeured over 750 soldiers (3 or 4 at a time with all their military gear) on their twenty-four-hour leaves, to and from Jerusalem and their checkpoints. We also collected signatures from Americans on petitions to President Nixon on the POW issue, delivered entertainers to a soldiers' rest home, chauffeured handicapped children and Hadassah nurses. When not behind the wheel, we conversed and conferred with family and friends, gaining deeper insight and understanding of the national mood. Our main assignment, chauffeuring soldiers, took us over 5,500 kilometers (4,000 miles) in the Judean desert and exposed us to the minds and feelings of our passengers. They, boys and girls and men, merely civilians wearing olive drab, included students, truck drivers, a civil engineer, a baker, a political science instructor, a hospital orderly, and a fashion designer. Youngsters in their army service, reservists in their mature years, single or family men—all agreed on preparedness as a basic requirement for survival. The economy was limping almost to the point of immobility because of the lack of exports, of tourists, and of enough manpower to make either possible. American contributions of desperately needed heavy artillery, shells and tanks were a tremendous boost to the national morale and certainly turned the tide on the battlefront.

On October 25, the *Pittsburgh Post-Gazette* carried a story on us under the heading "Tremendous Commitment." The editor of the "Better Living" section asked us to send back reports, which we did, and several were published. One piece that I dashed off between washing off the desert dust and getting ready for a social engagement in the evening I didn't share with the general public. Of all the twenty-one days plowing the road to Jericho, I feel most nostalgic about the Shabat our car broke down.

Marcia called in—while I was writing reports and attending to personal chores—to say that the car was stranded near the bullet-marked Notre Dame Hospice across from the New Gate of the Old City (the Jericho checkpoint). She had just returned from her second run and was suffering from an acute case of frustration and desperation. I immediately contacted my friendly auto repairman who, upon hearing my request for an immediate pickup, screamed at me in three languages. Didn't I know that there was a war on? That his tow truck was the only one left in the city still in civilian use, that it was noon on Friday and that Shabat was creeping up on us . . .? I was at Marcia's side within minutes by taxi and continued to make arrangements from the phone of the Arab Café, from which we could keep an eye on our unpatriotic Peugeot 504.

A municipality ombudsman came to investigate the problem, also a mechanic sent by him to make an emergency repair (unsuccessful). The precious minutes ticked away as we hoped for the tow truck's appearance and watched with envy our fellow drivers loading soldiers into their cars and returning from Jericho with others hopping out on leave. This was the low point in my morale. Finally the waiting became intolerable; I hailed a taxi and rushed to Hertz Rental. I was back at the scene behind the wheel of a Ford Escort within twenty minutes—in time to see my Peugeot disappear behind the open lot among the food stalls and donkey carts of East Jerusalem. Making a quick U turn, I raced through the main arteries of Jerusalem to Gassner's Auto Repair. The 504 preceded me, and when I arrived she was already on the hoist and a cotter pin was being inserted into her vital parts. It was now 2:00 P.M. and Gassner was about to close for the Shabat. I paid the equivalent of ten dollars, and we were both reassured and sent on our way with a cheerful "Get back on the road!" We did. In two cars now, we made one more round trip each. The soldier-chauffeuring never stopped for us.

I didn't think of myself as heroic or brave, not even as taking undue chances, though in fact I was. Having one foot in Jerusalem meant doing what everyone around me was doing, to the best of his or her possibilities. If folks in Pittsburgh thought that I did something especially commendable, I would hardly disavow it. As for me, I never felt so much an integral part of my community as I did during the time I ran the Ruttenberg-Ripp shuttle on the Jericho Road. If I had to do it over again, I would do exactly that.

As everyone else in Israel on November 19–22, 1977, I was glued to TV, watching the incredible events surrounding Sadat unfold. The possibility of his coming began to have a ring of reality two days before his actual arrival. From the moment that the planeload of journalists and security people landed at Ben Gurion Airport to the final disappearance of the Egyptian presidential plane into the Mediterranean sky, Israel was a State of Euphoria.

Home was the most advantageous place to be. When I slipped out for some groceries, and when I lunched with a friend, I carefully calculated every minute of the announced timetable. During every important event, I managed to be near a TV— nearly always my own—and I carried a transistor radio at all times. There seemed to be no end to the list of incredibles. Sadat's appearance and Begin's reception of him were matched for unexpectedness only by the Egyptians' Yom Kippur attack. That he should care now about the proper time of arrival—i.e., after the Shabat—was as bizarre as the very conception of his visit was genuine. This concern, as a matter of fact, was a signal that all points of protocol would be strictly adhered to, state of war or not: red carpet and fanfare, wreath laying, flags, honor guard and the Knesset appearance itself.

From the front balcony of my flat, I watched Sadat and his

entourage enter Jerusalem on Saturday evening; saw him pass through the valley to and from the Knesset and finally depart from Jerusalem on Tuesday. With an eye constantly on TV (without sound), and ears attuned to the radio for the English commentary, I witnessed four days of frenzied activity between Begin and Sadat and their aides in an unprecedented breakthrough for peace in the Middle East. The people of Israel were optimistic for the future and soberly accepted new facts in the relationship: de facto recognition and face-to-face talks, unthinkable only weeks earlier. They were also understandably cautious in their expectations.

The momentum so boldly and imaginatively initiated was to be continued. It seemed to all observers, however, that, while this point in history was pregnant with great possibilities, the delivery of real peace would not be an easy one. A healthy end product would come only after some complications and with no due date guaranteed. Sixteen months later a peace treaty was signed by Begin, Sadat and Carter on the White House lawn in Washington, D.C. While the terms of the treaty are being put into effect, Israelis and Egyptians are learning to cope with new and untried challenges of peace.

Shortly after the signing ceremony I attended a Passover Seder at our daughter's. In the narration we came to the portion that says: "We were once slaves in Egypt . . ." Whereupon we all thought and I ad-libbed: "And tomorrow we shall all be tourists there!"

Our two homes have much in common, and yet they are as different as can be. The one on Fifth Avenue is a combination of two consecutive two-bedroom apartments facing the hillside in the back, which gives us a 180-degree view of nature outdoors and complete privacy. With minor structural adjustments, we created an ideal apartment to suit our needs. Dad had his own room and bath; Harold has a large dining/living room area for his own private domain; Freda, her own office to work in on the occasions we need her. "His" kitchen provides, not only another cooking and serving facility (convenient at large parties), but also additional storage and a complete laundry. We both have every convenience we want, and, happily, we are able to house overnight guests comfortably as well. What was Dad's room is now an additional guest room, outfitted with the needs of nine grandchildren, from the youngest to the oldest.

Our front entrance is off a glass-enclosed foyer that brings the small atrium indoors (the tree there grows tall, to our eye level) and through which we see Fifth Avenue in the front. Our living/dining room also opens onto this area, giving us additional light, airiness and space.

The children long ago tagged our home as having that "well-lived-in look." Then as now, I find this a compliment. With our walls shamelessly overhung, sculpture and objets d'art in profusion everywhere, our Fifth Avenue apartment can hardly be called stuffy and formal. Some books, especially on art and those currently being read, are never in place on shelves; magazines and mail have a way of piling up relentlessly. The former are to be found wherever they are being read; on the latter I periodically employ a ruthless disposal method to keep from being submerged by an avalanche of papers—and vow to cut down on subscriptions.

I have every imaginable labor-saving device at my fingertips, but my most precious one is in the person of Edna Johnson, who helped us through the transition from house to penthouse and who continues to assist me in keeping my household running smoothly.

With a magnificent view over the Valley of the Cross,[32] our flat in Jerusalem has exposure on three sides and balconies on two, giving us plenty of air and light and a great deal to look out on. It boasts 110 square meters (the size of two-thirds of one of our Fifth Avenue apartments)—that's why we refer to it affectionately as our miniflat. To complement the furniture acquired there, we sent ourselves a liftful of household furnishings from the States, which enable me to keep house with all my accustomed conveniences and amenities. The flat also contains a collection of over 100 paintings, drawings and sculptures. Except for the fact that I occasionally aggravate myself over the neighbors' indifference to keeping the grounds and common elements properly maintained, I genuinely love keeping house in my Jerusalem miniflat. I get along well with all my neighbors, stateside and Israeli.

Being in Jerusalem in November, 1976, in no way interfered with my participation in the American presidential election. In fact my being there at that time formed a curious sequel to my first—and only—encounter with the candidate of my choice. Jimmie Carter, then Governor of Georgia, and I had met in Jerusalem about three and a half years earlier.

Granted that it is of vital concern to Israel who is in the White House, an American election has an added relevance to the Israelis who are also American citizens, dual citizenship being a precious advantage conferred on them. This time, too, there was a "Democrats-in-Israel" group, eighteen thousand strong, which had sent a delegate (Dr. Miron Sheshkin) to the Democratic National Convention with a voice and visibility. Americans in Jerusalem, whether also Israeli citizens, residents or tourists (my legal status), took an active part in the 1976 election, and most of them voted by absentee ballot—as I have. A victory celebration in the Hilton Hotel on the night of November 2 was their reward.

I could hardly get past the throngs of curious Yerushalmis who descended upon Democratic headquarters. The crowd, which included a great many students and young people, came to enjoy a carnival atmosphere and wall-to-wall TV sets. They noshed and read election literature. Flipping levers and popping names on and off, they practiced on the sample voting machine with much gusto. Only my friends and I knew that this marvel of American engineering was a product of Harold's AVM Company: this model and several others from AVM enable about half the American voters to exercise their political franchise.

I had reserved seats in the VIP room with friends who were leaders of "Democrats-in-Israel" and journalists (most of whom, like William Farrel of the *New York Times*, I knew personally). I was comfortable; but I gave up the vigil about 1:00 A.M. (6:00 P.M. in New York). I would have enjoyed the excitement of a postelection hoopla so far from the scene of the action, but the results were late coming in because of the seven-hour time difference. I therefore preferred to hear more definitive reports of trends and results during the night, in bed, via shortwave radio.

Jimmie Carter was a friend of a wealthy Atlanta supporter of the American College in Jerusalem, an institution of higher learning that I was at the time interested in promoting. A friend, Freddy Weisgal, was a key person in the affairs of the college; he and his wife, Jeanne, held a reception in their home in honor of the Governor of Georgia as a public relations event for the college. There were about fifty of us, and, while the college may not have benefited directly, we all had a marvelous time. The Governor was completely at ease, affable, and his famous smile even then was quite disarming. Speaking with an educated, well-modulated but noticeable drawl, Jimmie Carter was a great social success among us.

At one point in conversation with a few of us, he made a statement the substance of which later reverberated across America. Looking straight at us, he said, "I'm thinking of running for the presidency of the United States." I poked Harold in the rib and muttered, "He must be kidding!" He wasn't.

The next day, when Harold and I met him at the King David Hotel, we discovered that Jimmie Carter in May, 1973, had a firm intention towards the presidency. The two men went off together for a walking tour of the Old City, and I never found out for myself what Harold learned about our future President: that, among other things, he is utterly sincere and has a keen mind, like a sponge soaking up information. What he didn't know yet about Israel and the issues facing her, he readily absorbed from Freddie, Harold and others whom he met on this "private" visit in Israel. How he dealt with this briefing in subsequent years and what the quality of his performance as President was to be, I could in no way foretell. But, however his Jerusalem experience influenced his decisions vis-à-vis Israel, President Carter's Camp David coup and the Israeli-Egyptian Peace Treaty remain two of his brightest accomplishments.

We have subscription tickets for the Israel Philharmonic Orchestra and occupy seats located very similarly to those we hold in Heinz Hall in Pittsburgh. The sound of the orchestra may be different, and the people certainly are; programs, conductors and soloists often are the same. In both places, however, there are familiar faces around us. Attending concerts is one of our chief pleasures.

Being members of the International Board of the Israel Museum, Harold and I attend its May meetings in Jerusalem. I enjoy the ambience and the interchange of ideas when we meet art collectors and patrons who are Friends of the Museum, as well as its professional staff. Equally enjoyable are the occasional affairs we attend in Pittsburgh as Fellow (Harold) in the Carnegie Museum. Our interest in the work of the Jerusalem Foundation also brings us in contact with outstanding people who are active in support of the arts, such as dynamic Teddy Kollek, Mayor of Jerusalem, who is the moving spirit behind both the Israel Museum and the Jerusalem Foundation. The American-Israel Cultural Foundation (AICF), of which we were founding members in Pittsburgh and of which we are National Patrons, provides us with an additional level on which we meet people prominent in cultural and artistic pursuits. We have thus met Vera and Isaac Stern on a number of different occasions, most recently in a completely personal setting, one together with Dr. Frederick Dorian, whose acceptance as a Mishkenot guest Stern supported. Mishkenot is the Jerusalem VIP guest house for creative artists and scholars.

Once before, I helped arrange this coveted invitation, to Rene and Chaim Gross. During their residence, I had the opportunity to observe and hear two giants of the music world, Stern and Gina Bachauer, coach young, gifted Israelis and counsel them with regard to scholarships for continued studies abroad, usually under AICF auspices. The master classes took place in the Isaac Stern Music Center, on the grounds of Mishkenot. Bachauer died shortly after this visit in 1976.

Making Fritz Dorian's presence in Jerusalem possible was one of my most gratifying undertakings, even though at one point there was an element of heartbreak in it. There were a fat dossier of correspondence and many face-to-face talks; also endless arrangements to accommodate Fritz's physical handicap. When his wife died unexpectedly shortly before they were to have gone to Jerusalem, the project was jeopardized. In time, however, through a remarkable set of fortuitous circumstances, part domestic and part financial, he was able to plan ahead again. In the spring of 1978, he took up residence in Mishkenot[33] and became one of a long list of illustrious scholars, artists, musicians, writers and philosophers who have been guests at Mishkenot. Since Pablo Casals dedicated these unique "dwellings of tranquility" in Jerusalem's Yemin Moshe quarter in 1973, Simone de Beauvoir, Isaac Stern, Mstislav Rostropovich, Saul Bellow, Alexander Calder, Leon Uris and many other world-famed artists have stayed there. They interchanged ideas with their opposite numbers, communed with kindred souls and nurtured their creative genius.

Dorian plans a book for which his unique exposure to Israel, and to Jerusalem in particular, will have been essential. Among his numerous publications, his *Commitment to Culture* (University of Pittsburgh Press, 1964) is one that influenced the U.S. government's decision to establish the National Foundation on the Arts and the Humanities.

Giving a party with a celebrity as an "excuse" is just one of the ways I like to entertain. When Peter Frankl was the soloist and Lorin Maazel conducted the Philharmonic in Jerusalem, I gave a small reception at the miniflat in their honor. Just by chance, most of the guests had Pittsburgh connections; Peter himself had practiced on our Steinway in the penthouse and had been the center of the party we gave when he appeared with the Pittsburgh Symphony. Pittsburgh-reared Lorin, who is the Cleveland Symphony conductor and is famous on three continents, was a school chum of one of the guests in Jerusalem. In Pittsburgh, for many years, I have entertained gifted artists and Symphony personalities once a season in our home. Among them have been some busy globe-trotters: Annie Fischer, Znedek Macal, Itzhak Perlman, Vladimir Ashkenazy, Kyung-Wha Chung, David Bar Ilan, Mark Zeltser and Miriam Fried. In the course of three consecutive seasons recently, Miriam was our guest twice in Pittsburgh and once in Jerusalem, in both places receiving rave reviews and endearing herself to those who heard her play the violin and those who got a chance to meet her personally.

In both the miniflat and on Fifth Avenue, I lend my home to one of my favorite organizations now and then for a meeting, the art collection being the main focus of interest at such times. Sometimes I entertain especially for the purpose of presenting an artist of note, in or outside of the framework of the AICF. Harold and I get and give much pleasure with these parties; they seem to be smashing successes.

Our social life isn't all big parties and receptions. Simple dinner dates, quiet evenings at home with a friend or two, a coffee hour, a Sunday brunch for four or six—this is how most of our available free time is engaged. In Jerusalem, I entertain less around complete meals; and the Sunday brunch becomes a Shabat brunch or a Shabat afternoon coffee hour. Because Harold's Jerusalem time is more limited than mine, we live a more intensive social life there. We don't want to miss anyone, friends or family during the given period of time that we are in Jerusalem.

We have lost several dear friends in the States and in Jerusalem in recent years—par for the course!—and in America we find it less and less easy to make new enduring relationships. Not so in Jerusalem. In our later decades we are developing close, even intimate friendships, in all age categories, in spite of our being only part-time residents.

In Pittsburgh in recent years, a number of celebrations have taken place in our home, as I consider any milestone event more personal if celebrated at home. For our dear friends of long standing, Emma and Julius Finkelpearl, we gave a going-away party on the eve of their departure for San Francisco. In Esther Leavit's honor, a memorial gathering was held in our home, drawing together fifteen friends of hers who mourned her passing in quiet socializing—exactly the way she would have wanted it. For my brother-in-law Milton, who chose early retirement at sixty-three, we held a surprise party, the most welcome surprise of it all being the arrival of his and Harold's younger brother Stanley and sister-in-law from Washington especially for this occasion. For Sylvia and Bob Ilson, upon his retirement from the pulpit of Temple Sinai, we held a farewell reception. For Fritz Dorian, we gave a party in honor of his mission to Mishkenot. The guests, the gifts (if indicated), the menus and the high spirits all make splendid parties out of a simple excuse for getting together in family circles and in friendship. If I don't give a party for someone, I attend one. I love being a part of a personal celebration.

Epilogue

I am content with what is normally predictable in my life; I respond readily to the unforeseeable. I wouldn't live any other way. I cherish family and old friends and welcome new and younger people into my circle. I am pleased when persons the age of my own children get on with me so well, for they reinforce my self-confidence. I enjoy the children's and the grandchildren's nearness within manageable distances. Grandchildren-hopping has become a favorite pastime of mine. The life Harold and I have built for ourselves suits me just fine; I love shuttling between Pittsburgh and Jerusalem.

Now that I have told the story of my past and sketched the present, I can well afford to ponder on the future. I pray for health and friendships; joys multiplied; distresses soothed and family reunited. May all of us continue to have the strength and means to pursue these objectives! As for me, I shall emphasize satisfactions of my life; the pluses, past and present, shall be my props of the coming years. I have just slipped among the "aging" (using the term in its loosest sense). I intend to ease into senior citizenship gracefully and exercise it with all its privileges and rewards.

I am vitally concerned with the future, for this is where I shall spend the rest of my life.

Notes

1. *kashrut*—body of Jewish dietary laws.
2. Katalin—Since about age eight I've also been called Kitty, the name I am most popularly called currently.
3. UNRRA—United Nations Relief and Rehabilitation Administration.
4. *Inside U.S.A.*—Harper & Brothers, 1947, p. 615.
5. Pennsylvania Security League—a voluntary citizens' organization of liberals and noncommunist activists, with a strong social legislation platform and a program for organizing the unemployed and WPA workers of Pennsylvania.
6. NYA—New Deal agency providing jobs for students in their educational settings.
7. CCC—New Deal agency providing jobs for unemployed youth in landscape beautification and recreational facilities programs.
8. *As Steel Goes*—Yale University Press, 1940.
9. WPA—Works Progress Administration, a New Deal agency providing jobs for the unemployed.
10. Gesell and Ilg—Gesell, Arnold, and others (Frances Ilg, etc.), *First Five to Ten Years of Life*, Harper & Brothers, 1940; Gesell and Ilg, *The Child from Five to Ten*, Harper & Brothers, 1946.
11. Bernice Stanton—Bernice first came to work for me as a young high school girl. She rejoined us several times in the subsequent years as domestic employee, baby-sitter, and licensed practical nurse.
12. *shofar*—ram's horn. It is difficult to blow and get various sounds out of it. Jimmie blew with perfect results on every occasion for over a dozen years, even when he was away in school or on a job. He would simply fly home for the night and day.
13. Anne Frank book collection—English (USA), 1952; Dutch, 1947; Swedish, 1959; Turkish, 1958; Polish, 1960; Portuguese, n.d.; Slovak, 1960; Finnish, 1964; Italian, 1959; Hungarian, 1959; Czechoslovakian, 1957; Spanish, 1955; French, 1950; Russian, 1950; Japanese, n.d.; Hebrew, 1969; Greek, 1956; German, 1955.
14. Charles—staff attorney, National Labor Relations Board Washington, D.C. His wife Rhoda—reading specialist; recently earned her M.D. and is now resident in psychiatry.
James—telecommunications expert and mathematician, he has his own private consulting firm. His wife, Phyllis—M.A. reading specialist, now interested in gerontology.
Edward—rabbi of West End Synagogue, Nashville, Tennessee. His wife, Sarah—M.A. in English literature; now interested in finance.

Ellen—M.S.W. (social work); now interested in business and accountancy. Her husband, Harold—M.D. radiologist in private practice with group of associates.

15. YPO—Eligibility for membership in this organization was limited to men and women who have become chief executives of their companies before the age of forty and whose companies did at least $1 million worth of business annually (post–World War II evaluation of $1 million). YPO is alive and well.

16. . . . business, Israel and literary . . .—in Israel: America House in Tel Aviv, Rehovoth Instruments Company; Koor Industries; American-Israel Chamber of Commerce; Israel Aircraft Industries; Israel Military Industries.

17. Cuenca—ancient city from Roman times, now seat of the Spanish contemporary art movement.

18. Sharef—his major government posts: Secretary of the Provisional Government, Civil Service Commissioner, Director of Tax Office, Minister of Commerce and Industry, Minister of Housing.

19. Yad V'Shem—monument and documentation center for the 6 million martyrs who perished in the Holocaust.

20. Lon Kight—among the dozen non-Jewish friends and business associates whom we have entertained in Israel. Lately, our hospitality has been restricted to Jerusalem. Three others are Douglas Butchard of Perth, Scotland; Reginald Kemper of Pittsburgh (retired Rockwell official); and Ed Wisnewsky, long-time associate of Harold's who has also worked with him in Israel, now Executive Vice-President of AVM.

21. Passover—On the second day of this festival, a bundle of the newly harvested barley was brought to the Temple as a sacrifice, as a gift to God. And every day thereafter for forty-nine days, another sheaf of barley was brought to the Temple. Although sheaves of barley are not brought to the synagogue today, the forty-nine days of Omer are counted at services each day between Passover and the next festival, Shavu'ot, known as the Pentecost or the Feast of Weeks. Omer is a measure amounting to about a half gallon. Biblical reference for festivals: Leviticus 23.

22. Carol Elias—Carol and Kenny, young leaders in the Pittsburgh Jewish Community, attended a miniconference in our home and were sparked to make aliya (emigrate). They settled in Rosh Pina in 1972.

23. Yamit—in "Visit to Yamit," I reported to the *Jewish Chronicle* (December, 1976) on this northern Sinai Jewish settlement that became the object of controversy during subsequent peace talks.

24. Histadrut—Israel General Federation of Labor.

25. Our trials and tribulations . . .—an article by Harold detailing these problems, "Flat Circus," appeared in *Israel Magazine* in July, 1970.

26. Keren Hayesod—the organization for liaison with the diaspora—in fund-raising matters everywhere but the United States.

27. Kitty's Arab house—stands on property given to a sheik who helped Saladin win back Jerusalem from the Crusaders in the twelfth century.

28. . . . public servant, and as a successful author . . .—major posts held by Lord Samuel: colonial administrator in several areas and in different departments, Chief Censor for Palestine, Director of Palestine Broadcasting Service, in charge of training senior Israeli civil servants, senior lecturer at

Hebrew University, guest lecturer in universities abroad, including the University of Pittsburgh. Lord Samuel is author of short stories and of many books, articles, and monographs on administration. Two of the many are *A Life Time in Jerusalem* (autobiographical), Keter Publishing House, 1970, and *See How They Run* (about venerable institutions) The Woburn Press, 1976.

29. *O Jerusalem*—by Larry Collins and Dominique Lapierre, Simon & Schuster, 1972.

30. *The Arab Fisherman*—Its provenance is one of the most prominent in our collection: from Helena Rubinstein's.

31. . . . scheduled for October 1973—Outbreak of the Yom Kippur War did not cancel this exhibition but only postponed it; original poster and preview invitation showing change of dates became collector's items.

32. Valley of the Cross—Panorama includes dome of Hechal Schlomo (seat of the chief rabbinate), fourth-century Greek monastery, Hilton Hotel, Israel Museum complex, three government ministries, spanking new Paula Ben Gurion school, Givat Ram campus of Hebrew University and Mt. Herzl in the distance.

33. Mishkenot Sha'ananim—Artists, musicians, writers and scholars are invited to this guest house in Jerusalem for up to three months of residence under optimum conditions. The two buildings of Mishkenot were originally built as a private residence in the 1860s by Sir Moses Montefiore, who received for this purpose a generous legacy from the estate of his friend Judah Touro of New Orleans. The division of Jerusalem in 1948 resulted in the area's almost complete deterioration. Because it was on the border, many families abandoned it. Until 1967, only the very needy, refugees from Arab countries and from the Old City, made their homes there.

After the Six Day War, Teddy Kolleck and the Jerusalem Foundation decided to reconstruct the area, called Yemin Moshe. The two buildings became the VIP guest house, Mishkenot Sha'anamin (Dwellings of Tranquility).

Adjoining this unique artists' retreat is the Jerusalem Music Center. It was envisioned by Isaac Stern and guided through its preparatory stages by him and Teddy Kollek. Through financing by the Jerusalem Foundation and with a grant from the British Rothschild Foundation, the restoration of this gracious nineteenth-century stone building was made possible.

Index